Sophie Kay's

YOGURT COOKERY

YOGURT COOKERY

ANOTHER BEST-SELLING COOKERY VOLUME FROM H.P. BOOKS

Author: Mrs. Thomas Petros; Publisher: Helen Fisher;
Editors: Judi Ellingson, Carlene Tejada; Senior Editor: Jon
Latimer; Editor-in-Chief: Carl Shipman; Art Director: Don
Burton; Book Design: Tom Jakeway; Book Assembly: Tom
Jakeway, Mary Ann Kruger; Typography: Connie Brown,
Mary Kaye Fisher, Cindy Coatsworth; Food Stylist: Mable
Hoffman; Photography: George deGennaro Studios.

Published by H.P. Books, P O. Box 5367, Tucson, AZ 85703 602/888-2150
ISBN: Softcover, 0-912656-93-X; Hardcover, 0-912656-94-8
Library of Congress Catalog Card Number, 78-52271 ©1978 Fisher Publishing, Inc.
Printed in U.S.A.
Cover Photo: Baked Alaska Flambé, page 139

Sophie Kay

Sophie Kay loves yogurt! It's been a favorite in her family for years and she knows just about everything about this popular, natural food.

Sophie Kay is a nationally recognized home economist who conducted her own television cooking program in Chicago. She presently shares her recipes and cooking hints from the kitchen of a Milwaukee TV station and in various food and appliance commercials. Her degree in home economics and journalism is from Northwestern University.

Sophie Kay conducts cooking schools for television, radio, newspapers and schools. She is also the author of *Sophie Kay's Step by Step Cookbook*, *Sophie Kay's Family Cookbook*, *Menus From Around The World*, and *The Ideals Junior Chef Cookbook*.

The Story of Yogurt

THE STORY OF YOGURT

The recent rediscovery of yogurt has created a sensation in today's food world! But the story of yogurt probably began thousands of years ago in the Middle East. It is said that a nomad traveling the desert with his camel packed some milk in a goatskin bag. Hours later he found the milk had turned to a thick custard with a delicious tart flavor. The cause of this change was a mystery.

Yogurt kept its reputation as a mysterious, even miraculous food. It was used by early Greek physicians to cure stomach ailments, by Turks to cure insomnia and by Persian women as a face cream. About the time Columbus discovered America, King Francis I of France paid a small fortune for the secret of eternal life. It turned out to be yogurt.

Long life and yogurt have long been associated. It was the long life span of Bulgarians that led to the modern rediscovery of yogurt. Elie Metchnikoff, a Nobel Prize winning Russian bacteriologist, studied the Bulgarians and found that their main food was yogurt. He decided their longevity was due to the beneficial effects of yogurt bacteria on the human digestive system. Metchnikoff believed yogurt could lengthen any person's life span, so he ate a lot of it. He was not able to prove his point, but his researches made possible the large scale production of yogurt as we know it today.

NUTRITION

Yogurt is not a magic food, but it *is* an excellent supplement to a well-balanced diet. It's a good source of calcium, protein and riboflavin.

The calorie count of yogurt varies with the brand and the flavorings added. One 8-ounce cup of plain yogurt contains 120 to 170 calories. The same amount of yogurt with fruit added has 225 to 260 calories. Many physicians believe yogurt promotes the growth of beneficial intestinal bacteria. The therapeutic claims about yogurt are not proven.

WHAT YOU CAN DO WITH YOGURT

Not only is yogurt good for you, it tastes good too! Youngsters love it, teenagers think it's great and adults appreciate its food value. Yogurt is remarkably versatile in blending with a variety of foods in almost every kind of recipe. This book shows you how easy and fun it is to make your own yogurt. Your favorite foods will take on a new appearance and flavor as you create exciting new recipes with yogurt. Discover how to enhance the flavor of breads, cakes, casseroles, main dishes and vegetables! Enter the world of endless desserts and easy-to-make ice creams and sherbets! Enjoy Yogo-Cheese! It's easy to make and resembles cream cheese in flavor and texture, but has only half the calories. Begin the joy of *Yogurt Cookery* now!

Terms & Tools

Bacteria—Yogurt bacteria are friendly and manufacture large amounts of B vitamins. These beneficial bacteria are normally found in the intestinal tract of humans. They coagulate milk by causing an acid action. Yogurt gets its special flavor from these bacteria.

Culture—We refer to this as *Starter*.

Incubation—This is the period of several hours after adding starter to warm milk during which the milk stays warm, ferments and thickens to become yogurt.

Moisture Separation—The liquid that separates from the yogurt is sometimes called *whey*. It can be removed by placing white paper towels on the surface of the yogurt to absorb the liquid.

Starter—Plain yogurt, without flavorings or gelatin, is used to induce growth of beneficial bacteria in warm milk. This produces more yogurt. It is also called *culture*. You can use homemade plain yogurt or store-bought plain yogurt as starter. It is also available in freeze-dried packets in health food stores.

Yogurt—A thick custard-like dairy product made with the aid of beneficial bacteria. Starter or culture is added to warm milk and kept warm until the milk coagulates and reaches a semisolid state.

Utensils for making yogurt should be spotlessly clean. Use a large, heavy saucepan made of stainless steel, aluminum, enamel or heatproof glass, or coated with nonstick finish. A wire whisk is best for stirring yogurt to a creamy texture. The candy thermometer should measure 100°F (38°C) and above. Incubate the yogurt in one large or several individual covered containers made of glass, porcelain, earthenware or plastic. To maintain incubating temperature, use a thermal blanket, large towels, a thermos bottle, an insulated plastic carrying bag, a heating pad on low covered with a towel, an electric incubator, a thermal container, a slightly warm oven or a warming tray.

Buyer's Guide

Electric yogurt makers are designed to maintain the constant low heat necessary for growing the yogurt culture. All the electric machines tested were basically the same. They all produced the even temperature needed to make yogurt properly and they all worked well when tested. They varied only in the kinds of extras they include.

Each yogurt maker was tested several times with the Plain Yogurt recipe on page 13 and a variety of other recipes from this book. All the makers produced excellent yogurt. I was able to make delicious, sweet-tasting yogurt with an incubation time of only 3 hours. Several manufacturers suggest an incubation time of 10 hours. This is not necessary unless you want a very tart-tasting yogurt.

All the electric makers tested have handy jars and lids which can be stored in the refrigerator. Several manufacturers suggest using 1 tablespoon of starter for each jar. I used 3 tablespoons of starter for each quart or 5 cups of milk and poured the mix into individual cups. This worked well. Follow the manufacturer's directions if you use the freeze-dried culture included with some makers.

The nonelectric unit has a removable 1-1/2-quart container which can be used for storing yogurt in the refrigerator. This unit also worked well when tested with my Plain Yogurt recipe.

A compact 1-quart ice cream maker was also tested. It is designed to be placed in the freezer compartment of a refrigerator. I tested it with several of the frozen yogurt recipes, pages 150 to 159, and it produced very tasty frozen yogurt.

Contempra Automatic Yogurt Maker™
Contempra Industries, Inc., Tinton Falls, NJ 07753

This deluxe model has an automatic timer which turns off yogurt maker at a preset time. Manufacturer suggests putting starter into each jar. My tests gave the same results by putting 3 tablespoons starter directly into 5 cups of warm milk and pouring the mixture into the jars. This saves time and gives a more uniform product. This yogurt maker easily holds 5 cups warm milk with starter. Temperature is thermostatically controlled.

Wattage: 18 watts.
Capacity: 6 (8-oz.) clear glass jars with plastic lids.
Storage Size: 11" x 9" x 5" tall.
Cleaning: Glass jars are dishwasher safe. Base is not immersible.

Contempra Natural Yogurt Maker™
Contempra Industries, Inc., Tinton Falls, NJ 07753

This company's standard model has a special *Take-Out* dial which can be set as a reminder of when yogurt will be ready for refrigeration. It does not turn off the yogurt maker automatically. Manufacturer suggests putting starter into each jar. My tests gave the same results by putting 3 tablespoons starter directly into 5 cups of warm milk and pouring the mixture into the jars. This saves time and gives a more uniform product. This yogurt maker easily holds 5 cups warm milk with starter. Temperature is thermostatically controlled.

Wattage: 18 watts.
Capacity: 6 (8-oz.) clear glass jars with plastic lids.
Storage Size: 11" x 9" x 5" tall.
Cleaning: Glass jars are dishwasher safe. Base is not immersible.

Contempra Thriftee Yogurt Maker
Contempra Industries, Inc., Tinton Falls, NJ 07753

This model has no timer, dial or cover. Manufacturer suggests putting starter into each jar. My tests gave the same results by putting 3 tablespoons starter directly into 5 cups warm milk and pouring the mixture into the jars. This saves time and gives a more uniform product. This yogurt maker easily holds 5 cups warm milk with starter. Temperature is thermostatically controlled.

Wattage: 18 watts.
Capacity: 6 (8-oz.) clear glass jars with plastic lids.
Storage Size: 11" x 9" x 5" tall.
Cleaning: Glass jars are dishwasher safe. Base is not immersible.

Hamilton Beach Culture Center Electric Yogurt Maker
Hamilton Beach, Div. of Scovill, Waterbury, CT 06720

This unit has a time and consistency reminder. An hour reminder guide can be set to help you remember when the yogurt will be ready for refrigeration. It does not turn off the yogurt maker automatically. This unit comes with a tinted cover and a handy plastic measuring spoon thermometer to let you know exactly when temperature is right for adding yogurt starter. Manufacturer suggests using 1 quart milk. In testing I found yogurt maker can easily hold 5 cups warm milk with starter. Temperature is thermostatically controlled.

Wattage: 28 watts.
Capacity: 6 (8-oz.) clear glass jars with plastic lids.

Storage Size: 10" x 7" x 5" tall.
Cleaning: Glass jars and cover go in top shelf of dishwasher. Base is not immersible.

Salton Ice Cream Machine™
Salton, Inc., Bronx, NY 10462

This compact, convenient unit makes ice cream or frozen yogurt in the freezer compartment of your refrigerator. Your freezer must be cold enough to keep ice cream frozen in order for this unit to work properly. Mixture must be chilled 2 hours in refrigerator before placing into the unit. The unit is set in the freezer and plugged into an outlet. The ice cream machine stirs and aerates the ice cream mix as it freezes. A fan on top pulls cold air through vents and replaces the salt-and-ice method used in conventional electric ice cream makers.

Wattage: 36 watts.
Cord: Special 7-1/2-foot cord extends from freezer and plugs into wall outlet.

Cleaning: Power unit is not immersible. Base, stirrer and lid should be washed by hand and dried thoroughly before storing.

Salton Yogurt Maker
Salton, Inc., Bronx, NY 10462

This thermostatically controlled electric unit has a special *Time-Out* dial to remind you when to remove yogurt and place it in the refrigerator. It does not turn off the yogurt maker automatically. A handy plastic measuring spoon thermometer that comes with the maker lets you know exactly when temperature is right for adding the yogurt starter.

Wattage: 25 watts.
Capacity: 5 (6-oz.) white glass jars with capacity lids.

Storage Size: 16" x 3-1/2" x 5" tall.
Cleaning: Glass jars and spoon thermometer are dishwasher safe. The body of the yogurt maker is not immersible.

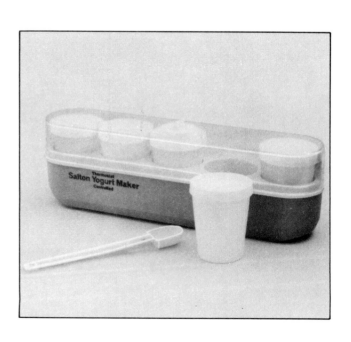

West Bend® Yogurt Maker
The West Bend Company, West Bend, WI 53097

This maker has six serving jars that sit on a removable plastic tray that can be placed in the refrigerator. The dial in the plastic lid can be set to remind you when yogurt is ready for refrigeration. It does not turn off the yogurt maker automatically. Manufacturer suggests putting starter into each jar. This machine has just gone into production and was unavailable for testing at the time of this writing. Temperature is thermostatically controlled.

Wattage: 18 watts.

Capacity: 6 (8-oz.) clear glass jars with snap-on plastic lids.

Cleaning: Glass jars and plastic tray are dishwasher safe. Base is not immersible.

Yogotherm® Incubator
International Yogurt Company, Los Angeles, CA 90069

This is a nonelectric incubating unit. Warm milk mixed with starter is poured into a plastic container. The container is placed into the thermal case which maintains proper temperature for incubation. This unit can also be used to incubate kefir, acidophilus and buttermilk or sour cream cultures. The container can be stored in refrigerator. Follow manufacturer's instructions.

Capacity: 1-1/2 to 2 quarts.   **Storage Size:** 8" diameter by 9".

One reason why some people do not have success making yogurt is their utensils are not spotlessly clean. Even though the pan you heat milk in and your incubating containers look clean, scrub them thoroughly before making yogurt. A tiny scorch mark on a pan or an almost invisible ring on an incubating container can interfere with the yogurt making process.

How To Make Yogurt

There are 5 basic types of yogurt:

- Plain yogurt without flavoring or fruit.
- Flavored yogurt without fruit.
- Flavored yogurt with fruit or vegetables. *Sundae-style* yogurt has fruit at the bottom of the container with plain or flavored yogurt on top. *Blended-style* yogurt, also called Swiss-style or French-style yogurt, has fruit and yogurt blended.
- Frozen yogurt has the texture of creamy ice cream or sherbet, and a slight tang. It makes beautiful parfaits, sundaes or popsicles.
- Yogurt cheese is a solid, smooth-textured white cheese resembling cream cheese.

When recipes in this book call for yogurt, use homemade or store-bought yogurt. Homemade yogurt is usually sweeter than store-bought yogurt.

With a yogurt maker you can make a variety of flavored yogurts at one time. Heat 2 to 3 quarts of milk; make 1 large container of plain yogurt and several individual cups of different flavored yogurts.

If a yogurt maker is not available, make individual servings in small jars or glasses. Put the jars of warm milk with starter in a 2-inch deep baking pan. Turn an electric heating pad on low and place a cooling rack on the pad. Set the baking pan with the jars or glasses on the rack. Spoon the flavorings into the bottom of each container, fill with the prepared milk and cover with a small baking sheet. Wrap with a blanket or a large towel and incubate.

THE 3 T's OF YOGURT MAKING

Make perfect yogurt every time by closely watching the temperatures during these 3 stages.

- **Temperature for Heating**—Bring milk to 190° to 210°F (90° to 99°C) or just under boiling. The milk will be covered with tiny bubbles under the protein film. This temperature destroys undesirable organisms which may prevent coagulation. Heating the milk helps prepare it for rapid fermentation.
- **Temperature for Cooling**—Cool milk to 110° to 115°F (43° to 46°C). This is the ideal temperature for adding the yogurt starter. Before we had thermometers, a person making yogurt dipped a finger into the warm milk and counted to 20. If the person could stand the heat, the milk was ready.

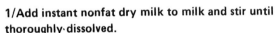

1/Add instant nonfat dry milk to milk and stir until thoroughly dissolved.

2/Attach candy thermometer to saucepan. Heat milk over low heat to just below boiling, 190° to 210°F (90° to 99°C). Remove milk from heat. Cool to about 110°F (43°C).

3/The yogurt starter should be at room temperature. Remove any protein film from the warm milk. Stir starter until creamy, and mix about 1/3 cup of the warm milk into the starter.

• **Temperature for Incubating**—This temperature can range from 105° to 120°F (41° to 48°C). Below 105°F (41°C) the bacteria in the starter become less active and take longer to grow. Temperatures over 120°F (48°C) will destroy the bacteria. I use 110°F (43°C) which works the best for me.

THE YOGURT STARTER

Yogurt starter, which is simply fresh unflavored yogurt, should be at room temperature. Stir a little of the warm milk into the starter to thin it down, making it easier to blend into the milk. Stir the starter mixture into the remaining warm milk and pour into the incubating containers. While kept at a constant temperature, the bacteria in the yogurt starter multiply, breaking up the sugar lactose in the milk to form lactic acid. The lactic acid turns the milk into the custard-like consistency called *yogurt*.

If you use the freeze-dried culture available in health food stores for your starter, follow the manufacturer's instructions on the packet.

Make sure your starter is not flavored and does not contain gelatin.

ACTIVITY TEST

Some store-bought yogurts are pasteurized after the yogurt-making process. This prolongs their shelf life but kills the live bacteria which are necessary if the yogurt is to be used as a starter. Test for

live bacteria by stirring 2 tablespoons of the yogurt into a cup of warmed milk, about 110°F (43°C). Incubate for a few hours or overnight. If the milk has thickened and set, the yogurt may be used as a starter. If the milk has not thickened, the yogurt does not contain live bacteria.

CONTROLLING THE TASTE

The taste of yogurt ranges from sweet to extremely tart. The temperature of the milk when the starter is added and the length of incubation time both influence the taste.

The warmer the milk is within the range of 110° to 115°F (43° to 46°C) when the starter is added, the more tart the yogurt will be. The cooler the milk is within the same range, the sweeter the yogurt. Long incubation time results in tart yogurt. Short incubation time produces sweet yogurt. Yogurt also becomes more tart the longer it is stored.

STORAGE

Plain yogurt will keep up to 4 weeks in the refrigerator. Yogurt with fruit or vegetables will keep up to 1 week. Always keep stored yogurt covered. Moisture separation will form once you cut into the yogurt. Spoon this liquid out. Or place several layers of white paper towels over the yogurt to absorb the liquid; repeat if necessary. This produces a thick yogurt. If you stir the moisture separation back into the yogurt, the yogurt will not be firm again unless it contains gelatin.

4/Stir yogurt starter and warm milk mixture into the remaining warm milk. Mix well.

5/To make individual servings, pour warm milk with starter into small containers with covers. Incubate in yogurt maker or with another incubating method.

6/You can also pour warm milk with starter into a large container with a cover.

7/Wrap warm milk with starter in a thermal blanket and incubate in a warm place at a constant temperature of about 110°F (43°C) for 3 to 4 hours. Do not disturb during incubation. Milk will coagulate and reach a semisolid state.

8/Check yogurt after incubating 3 hours. If yogurt is not set, incubate another hour. As soon as yogurt is set, refrigerate at least 6 hours before serving. When chilled, yogurt will have a thick custard-like consistency.

Plain Yogurt

My favorite for most of the recipes in this cookbook.

1 quart 2% low-fat or skim milk
1/2 cup instant nonfat dry milk

3 tablespoons plain yogurt, room temperature

Put 1 cup low-fat or skim milk in a small bowl. Add dry milk and stir until dissolved. Rinse a 2-quart saucepan with water to help prevent the milk from sticking and pour in remaining 3 cups milk and dissolved dry milk. Mix well. Attach thermometer and heat milk over low heat to 190°F to 210°F (90° to 99°C). Remove from heat and cool to 110°F (43°C). Remove protein film from top of milk. In a small bowl, stir yogurt until creamy. Mix about 1/3 cup warm milk into yogurt. Blend until smooth. Stir yogurt-milk mixture into remaining milk. Mix well. Pour into a 1-1/2 quart container or individual containers. Cover. Incubate 3 to 4 hours at a constant temperature of about 110°F (43°C). Do not disturb during incubation. After 3 hours, gently shake mixture to see if it is firm. If not firm, let stand 1 more hour and check again. Refrigerate as soon as yogurt begins to set. Chill at least 6 hours before serving. For a thicker yogurt, place several layers of white paper towels on top of chilled yogurt to absorb moisture separation. Makes about 1 quart. To make 2, 3, or 4 quarts yogurt, increase ingredient amounts proportionately. Incubation time will be the same.

Variation
Substitute skim milk for low-fat milk.

Secrets For Perfect Yogurt

PROBLEM	WHY	WHAT TO DO
Doesn't thicken	Milk was too hot or too cool when starter was added	Add starter when milk is 110° to 115°F (43° to 46°C).
	Not enough starter added	Add 3 tablespoons yogurt starter per quart.
	Incubating temperature too low or too high	Incubate at 105° to 120°F (41° to 48°C).
		Incubate longer; it will eventually thicken but will be tart.
	Milk was moved or stirred	Place in a quiet location where it will not be disturbed.
	Starter was inactive	Test yogurt used as starter for live bacteria; see Activity Test, page 11.
Too thin	Starter getting weak	Buy new starter.
	Not enough instant nonfat dry milk added	Add more instant nonfat dry milk.
Too tart	Incubated too long	Reduce incubation time.
		Refrigerate after 3 to 4 hours, as soon as milk begins to thicken. Milk will continue to thicken in refrigerator.
Too much moisture separation	Incubated too long	Reduce incubation time.
	Bumped, moved or stirred	Place in a quiet location where it will not be disturbed.
		Do not move or stir. The slightest movement can cause moisture separation.

Whole Milk Yogurt

Good basic yogurt with a rich taste.

1 quart whole milk
3 tablespoons plain yogurt, room temperature

Rinse a 2-quart saucepan with water. Pour in milk. Attach thermometer and heat milk over low heat to 190° to 210°F (90° to 99°C). Remove from heat and cool to 110°F (43°C). Remove protein film from top of milk. In a small bowl, stir yogurt until creamy. Mix about 1/3 cup warm milk into yogurt. Blend until smooth. Stir yogurt-milk mixture into remaining milk. Mix well. Pour into a 1-1/2-quart container or individual containers. Cover. Incubate 3 to 4 hours at a constant temperature of about 110°F (43°C). Do not disturb during incubation. After 3 hours, gently shake mixture to see if it is firm. If not firm, let stand 1 more hour and check again. Refrigerate as soon as yogurt begins to set. Chill at least 6 hours before serving. Makes about 1 quart.

Low-Fat Milk Yogurt

Quick yogurt for those in a hurry.

1 quart water
2 cups instant nonfat dry milk

3 tablespoons plain yogurt, room temperature

Place water in 2-quart saucepan. Attach thermometer and heat to 120°F (49°C). Add dry milk and stir until dissolved. In a small bowl, stir yogurt until creamy. Mix about 1/3 cup warm milk mixture into yogurt. Stir yogurt-milk mixture into remaining milk. Mix well. Pour into a 1-1/2-quart container or individual containers. Cover. Incubate 3 to 4 hours at a constant temperature of about 110°F (43°C). Do not disturb during incubation. After 3 hours, remove cover and gently shake mixture to see if it is firm. If not firm, let stand 1 more hour and check again. Refrigerate as soon as yogurt begins to set. Chill at least 6 hours before serving. Makes about 1 quart.

Use a nonstick spray on the saucepan the milk is heated in to prevent the milk from sticking to the pan. It makes cleaning up easier.

Half-and-Half Yogurt

Great for malts, shakes and other beverages.

2 cups whole milk
2 cups half-and-half

3 tablespoons plain yogurt, room temperature

Rinse a 2-quart saucepan with water. Pour in milk and half-and-half. Mix well. Attach thermometer and heat milk over low heat to 190° to 210°F (90° to 99°C). Remove from heat and cool to 110°F (43°C). Remove protein film from top of milk. In a small bowl, stir yogurt until creamy. Mix about 1/3 cup warm milk mixture into yogurt. Blend until smooth. Stir yogurt-milk mixture into remaining milk. Mix well. Pour into a 1-1/2-quart container or individual containers. Cover. Incubate 3 to 4 hours at a constant temperature of about 110°F (43°C). Do not disturb during incubation. After 3 hours, remove cover and gently shake mixture to see if it is firm. If not firm, let stand 1 more hour and check again. Refrigerate as soon as yogurt begins to set. Chill at least 6 hours before serving. Makes about 1 quart.

Whipping Cream Yogurt

Serve this as a dessert with fruit or use in dessert recipes.

1 teaspoon unflavored gelatin
3 cups whole milk

1 cup whipping cream
3 tablespoons plain yogurt, room temperature

Soften gelatin by soaking it in 1/4 cup milk for about 5 minutes. Stir a little more milk into the gelatin-milk mixture. Rinse a 2-quart saucepan with water. Pour remaining milk, whipping cream and gelatin-milk mixture into saucepan. Mix well. Attach thermometer and heat milk over low heat to 190° to 210°F (90° to 99°C). Remove from heat and cool to 110°F (43°C). Remove protein film from top of milk. In a small bowl, stir yogurt until creamy. Mix about 1/3 cup warm milk mixture into yogurt. Blend until smooth. Stir yogurt-milk mixture into remaining milk. Mix well. Pour into a 1-1/2-quart container or individual containers. Cover. Incubate 3 to 4 hours at a constant temperature of about 110°F (43°C). Do not disturb during incubation. After 3 hours, remove cover and gently shake mixture to see if it is firm. If not firm, let stand 1 more hour and check again. Refrigerate as soon as yogurt begins to set. Chill at least 6 hours before serving. Makes about 1 quart.

If necessary, when heating the milk on an electric burner, use a diffusing ring to disperse the heat evenly. This will help prevent the milk from sticking to the bottom of the pan.

Evaporated Milk Yogurt

Rich and delicious!

1 quart 2% low-fat or whole milk
1 (13-oz.) can low-fat or regular
  evaporated milk

1/4 cup plain yogurt, room temperature

Rinse a 2-quart saucepan with water. Pour in low-fat or whole milk and evaporated milk. Mix well. Attach thermometer and heat milk over low heat to 190° to 210°F (90° to 99°C). Remove from heat and cool to 110°F (43°C). Remove protein film from top of milk. In a small bowl, stir yogurt until creamy. Mix about 1/3 cup warm milk mixture into yogurt. Blend until smooth. Stir yogurt-milk mixture into remaining milk. Mix well. Pour into a 1-1/2-quart container or individual containers. Cover. Incubate 3 to 4 hours at a constant temperature of about 110°F (43°C). Do not disturb during incubation. After 3 hours, remove cover and gently shake mixture to see if it is firm. If not firm, let stand 1 more hour and check again. Refrigerate as soon as yogurt begins to set. Chill at least 6 hours before serving. Makes about 1 quart.

Variation

Substitute 3 cups water for 1 quart 2% low-fat or whole milk, and use 2 (13-oz.) cans evaporated milk instead of 1 can.

Plain Yogurt With Gelatin

Ideal for making Swiss-style yogurt.

1 envelope unflavored gelatin
2 tablespoons cold water
1 quart 2% low-fat or skim milk

1/3 cup instant nonfat dry milk
3 tablespoons plain yogurt, room temperature

In a small cup, soften gelatin in cold water about 5 minutes. Pour 1 cup of the low-fat or skim milk in a bowl. Add dry milk. Stir until dissolved. Rinse a 2-quart saucepan with water. Pour in remaining 3 cups milk, dissolved dry milk and softened gelatin. Mix well. Attach thermometer and heat milk over low heat to 190° to 210°F (90° to 99°C). Remove from heat and cool to 110°F (43°C). Remove protein film from top of milk. In a small bowl, stir yogurt until creamy. Mix about 1/3 cup warm milk mixture into yogurt. Blend until smooth. Stir yogurt-milk mixture into remaining milk. Mix well. Pour into a 1-1/2-quart container or individual containers. Cover. Incubate 3 to 4 hours at a constant temperature of about 110°F (43°C). Do not disturb during incubation. After 3 hours, remove cover and gently shake mixture to see if it is firm. If not firm, let stand 1 more hour and check again. Refrigerate as soon as yogurt begins to set. Chill at least 6 hours before serving. To make Flavored Yogurt, page 18, refrigerate set yogurt 15 minutes. Stir until creamy. Fold in fruit or flavorings. Cover and refrigerate at least 6 hours. Makes about 1 quart.

Yogurt With Cornstarch

Cornstarch makes yogurt smoother and creamier.

1 quart 2% low-fat or skim milk
1/3 cup instant nonfat dry milk
1 tablespoon cornstarch

2 tablespoons cold water
3 tablespoons plain yogurt, room temperature

Pour 1 cup of low-fat or skim milk in a small bowl. Add dry milk. Stir until dissolved. Rinse a 2-quart saucepan with water. Pour in remaining 3 cups milk and dissolved dry milk. Mix well. Attach thermometer and heat milk over low heat to 200°F (93°C). Dissolve cornstarch in cold water. Stir into milk. Mix well. Heat milk-cornstarch mixture over low heat to 210°F (99°C). Remove from heat and cool to 110°F (43°C). Remove protein film from top of milk. In a small bowl, stir yogurt until creamy. Mix about 1/3 cup warm milk mixture into yogurt. Blend until smooth. Stir yogurt-milk mixture into remaining milk. Mix well. Pour into a 1-1/2-quart container or individual containers. Cover. Incubate 3 to 4 hours at a constant temperature of about 110°F (43°C). Do not disturb during incubation. After 3 hours, remove cover and gently shake mixture to see if it is firm. If not firm, let stand 1 more hour and check again. Refrigerate as soon as yogurt begins to set. Chill at least 6 hours before serving. Makes about 1 quart.

Sweet Vanilla Yogurt

Excellent for dessert!

3 cups warm water (120°F, 50°C)
1 cup instant nonfat dry milk
1/2 cup sweetened condensed milk

1/4 cup plain yogurt, room temperature
1/2 teaspoon vanilla extract

In a small bowl, place warm water, dry milk, sweetened condensed milk and yogurt. Mix with electric mixer on low speed until blended. Pour into a 1-1/2-quart container or individual containers. Cover. Incubate 3 to 4 hours at a constant temperature of about 110°F (43°C). Do not disturb during incubation. After 3 hours, remove cover and gently shake mixture to see if it is firm. If not firm, let stand 1 more hour and check again. Refrigerate as soon as yogurt begins to set. Chill at least 6 hours before serving. Makes about 1 quart.

Whenever you make yogurt, remember to set aside about 3 tablespoons of yogurt for starter for the next time. The starter will keep up to 4 weeks in the refrigerator.

Flavored Yogurts

The amounts on this chart make a 1-cup serving. To make more, multiply by the number of cups desired. Place flavorings in the bottom of small containers. Add enough warm milk with starter to fill cups to about 1/2 inch from top. Cover and incubate. Make several different flavors at one time with different flavorings in the bottom of each cup.

To make blended-style or Swiss-style yogurt, place 1 tablespoon any flavor thick preserves in an individual container; add warm milk with starter, mix well and incubate. You can also stir your favorite flavorings into plain yogurt from your market.

28 Varieties of Flavored Yogurts

VARIETY	INGREDIENTS TO MAKE 1 CUP	ADDITIONAL INSTRUCTIONS
Almond	1 tablespoon finely chopped almonds 1 tablespoon brown sugar 10 drops almond extract	
Apple	1/4 small Delicious apple 2 teaspoons sugar	Do not peel apple. Cut in thin slices; halve slices.
Applesauce	2 tablespoons chunky applesauce 2 teaspoons sugar	Sprinkle with dash of cinnamon before serving.
Apricot	3 dried apricots, chopped 2 teaspoons sugar	Sprinkle with dash of cloves before serving.
Banana	2 tablespoons honey 2 drops banana extract	
Blueberry	1 tablespoon thick blueberry preserves	
Carrot	3 tablespoons grated raw carrot Dash salt	Drain grated carrot well.
Cherry	1 tablespoon thick cherry preserves or 6 cherries pitted and halved 2 teaspoons sugar	
Chocolate	1-1/2 tablespoons chocolate syrup 1 teaspoon shaved chocolate, if desired	
Cocoa	1 tablespoon Nestlé® Quik chocolate flavor	
Coffee	1 teaspoon instant coffee powder 1/4 teaspoon hot water 1 tablespoon sugar	Dissolve coffee in hot water in individual cup before adding sugar.
Cucumber	3 tablespoons grated cucumber 1/8 teaspoon dill weed Dash garlic salt	Drain grated cucumber well.
Garden Salad	1 tablespoon grated raw carrot 1 tablespoon grated cucumber 1 tablespoon minced radish 1/2 teaspoon snipped chives Pinch dill weed Dash garlic salt	Drain grated carrot and grated cucumber well.

VARIETY	INGREDIENTS TO MAKE 1 CUP	ADDITIONAL INSTRUCTIONS
Honey	1 tablespoon honey	
Lemon	2 teaspoons fresh lemon juice 2 teaspoons sugar	Lemon Yogurt is best made with Plain Yogurt With Gelatin, page 16.
Orange	2 tablespoons orange marmalade or 2 tablespoons chopped fresh orange sections 2 teaspoons sugar	
Peach	1 tablespoon thick peach preserves or 5 thin slices fresh peeled peach 2 teaspoons sugar or 1/2 dried peach half, chopped	If using fresh peach slices, cut in half
Peanut Butter	1 tablespoon plain or crunchy peanut butter	
Pear	5 thin slices pear 2 teaspoons sugar	Peel pear, if desired. Cut pear slices in half.
Peppermint	2 hard peppermint candies 2 drops peppermint extract	Crush peppermint candies.
Pineapple-Coconut	1 tablespoon pineapple juice concentrate 1 tablespoon flaked coconut 1 tablespoon pineapple preserves	Place ingredients in bottom of individual cup in the order given.
Plum	2 small fresh plums, sliced 2 teaspoons sugar	Peel plums, if desired.
Prune	2 prunes, chopped 2 teaspoons sugar	
Raisin	2 tablespoons golden raisins	Cut raisins in half.
Raspberry	1 tablespoon thick raspberry preserves	
Strawberry	1 tablespoon thick strawberry preserves or 2 tablespoons sliced strawberries 2 teaspoons sugar	
Tomato Juice	1 tablespoon tomato juice Dash garlic salt	If desired, add a drop of Tabasco® sauce before serving.
Vanilla	1 teaspoon vanilla extract 2 to 3 teaspoons sugar	

Breakfast & Brunch

Yogurt is right at home on the breakfast table. Stir it into farina or other hot cereals for added taste and nutrition. In Triple Treat Breakfast Cereal, yogurt tops your favorite cold cereal. I use honey-flavored yogurt, but fruit-flavored yogurt or even plain yogurt adds zip. Stir yogurt with a wire whisk to make it creamy before spooning it over cereals.

Surprise everyone on Sunday morning with Fluffy Pancakes made with yogurt. Honey-flavored yogurt is a nifty topping for pancakes, waffles or French toast. Of course, the perfect ham and eggs breakfast has to have freshly baked muffins. In this section you'll find 3 exquisite muffin recipes.

On holidays or special occasions, Surprise Apple Coffeecake is a delightfully moist sweet cake with 3 delicious layers of fruit and nuts. Entertain with Ham Quiche Lorraine or Spinach Soufflé Squares and you'll have everyone asking for the recipe! The quiche, a main-dish cheese and ham pie, can also be served for dinner.

PANCAKE BREAKFAST
Fresh Orange Juice
Fluffy Pancakes, page 28
Warm Maple Syrup
Hickory Smoked Bacon
Spiced Coffee or Tea

ROMAN BRUNCH
Frittata, page 29
Hot Garlic Bread
Prosciutto With Melon
Cappuccino

PATIO BRUNCH
Red Riding Hood, page 37
Spinach Soufflé Squares, page 30
Petite Crusty Rolls
Butter Curls
Honeydew Melon

SUNSHINE BREAKFAST
Chilled Vegetable Juice
Creamy Oatmeal, page 25
Sunnyside Eggs
Blueberry Muffins, page 26
Coffee

Surprise Apple Coffeecake

An irresistible trio of raisins, nuts and apples.

Raisin-Nut Filling, see below
2 cups all-purpose flour
1 teaspoon baking powder
1 teaspoon baking soda
1/2 teaspoon salt
1/2 cup plus 1 tablespoon butter or margarine

1 cup sugar
2 eggs
1 teaspoon vanilla extract
1 cup plain yogurt, room temperature
2 medium apples, peeled and sliced

Raisin-Nut Filling:
1/2 cup raisins
1/2 cup chopped walnuts

1/2 cup sugar
1 tablespoon cinnamon

Prepare Raisin-Nut Filling. Preheat oven to 375°F (190°C). Generously grease a 9-inch angelfood cake pan with removable bottom. Sift together flour, baking powder, baking soda and salt. Cream butter or margarine in a large bowl. Gradually add sugar. Beat until light and fluffy. Add eggs 1 at a time, beating well after each addition. Stir in vanilla. Add flour mixture alternately with yogurt to creamed mixture, beginning and ending with flour mixture. Spread half the batter in prepared pan. Arrange sliced apples over the batter. Sprinkle half the Raisin-Nut Filling over apples. Spread remaining batter over filling. Lightly press remaining Raisin-Nut Filling into batter. Bake 40 to 45 minutes until cake springs back when lightly touched. Cool in pan on wire rack about 30 minutes. Loosen edges and remove cake from pan. Makes one coffeecake.

Raisin-Nut Filling:
Combine raisins, walnuts, sugar and cinnamon in a small bowl. Mix well.

Peach Puffs

Pretty as a picture.

1 (13-3/4-oz.) pkg. hot roll mix
1/4 cup warm water (110°F, 45°C)
1/4 cup sugar

1/2 cup plain yogurt, room temperature
1 egg
1/4 cup peach preserves

Preheat oven to 375°F (190°C). Generously grease muffin pans. In a large bowl, dissolve yeast from hot roll mix in warm water. Stir in sugar, yogurt and egg. Add flour mixture from hot roll mix. Blend well. Cover and let rise in a warm place about 45 minutes until doubled in bulk. On a generously floured surface, knead dough 1 to 2 minutes until smooth. Divide dough into 12 equal parts. Put dough into muffin cups, pressing toward bottom and sides of muffin cups. Put about 1 teaspoon peach preserves in each center. Cover and let rise in a warm place 35 to 45 minutes until doubled in bulk. Bake 15 to 25 minutes until golden brown. Remove from muffin pans. Serve warm. Makes 12 puffs.

Criss-Cross Caramel Coffeecake

The ideal coffeecake for your buffet brunch.

5-1/2 to 6 cups all-purpose flour
1 teaspoon salt
2 pkgs. active dry yeast
1/2 cup sugar
1/4 cup warm water, about 110°F, 45°C
2 cups plain yogurt, room temperature

1/2 cup butter or margarine, softened
2 eggs
1 teaspoon vanilla extract
Caramel Crunch Filling, see below
Last-Minute Icing, see below

Caramel Crunch Filling:
1/2 cup light-brown sugar, firmly packed
1/2 cup all-purpose flour
Dash salt

1/2 teaspoon cinnamon
4 tablespoons butter or margarine
1/4 cup chopped walnuts

Last-Minute Icing:
1 cup sifted powdered sugar
2 tablespoons plain yogurt, room temperature

1/2 teaspoon grated orange peel

Set aside 1/2 cup of flour for kneading. In a medium bowl, mix remaining flour and salt. In a large bowl, dissolve yeast and sugar in warm water. Stir yogurt until creamy. Blend yogurt into yeast mixture. Beat in 2 cups flour-salt mixture. Add butter or margarine, eggs and vanilla. Blend well. By hand, beat in enough remaining flour-salt mixture to make a firm dough. Sprinkle reserved 1/2 cup flour on a flat surface. Knead dough about 8 to 10 minutes until smooth and elastic. Lightly butter large bowl. Put dough in bowl and turn dough to butter top. Cover and let rise in a warm place about 1 to 1-1/2 hours until doubled in bulk. Cut dough in half. Preheat oven to 375°F (190°C). Generously grease a baking sheet. Set aside. On a lightly floured surface, punch down half of dough. Cover and let stand 10 minutes. Prepare Caramel Crunch Filling. Roll out dough to an 8" x 18" rectangle. Spread Caramel Crunch Filling lengthwise along the center third of rectangle. With a scissors or sharp knife, cut slashes 1 inch apart along each side of filling. Fold strips crisscross fashion at an angle across filling. Carefully place cake on prepared baking sheet. If necessary, form cake into a crescent so it will fit on baking sheet. Repeat for other half of dough. Cover and let rise in a warm place about 45 minutes until doubled in bulk. Bake about 30 minutes until golden brown. Cool. Prepare Last-Minute Icing and brush over coffeecake. Makes 2 coffeecakes.

Caramel Crunch Filling:
In a medium bowl, mix brown sugar, flour, salt and cinnamon. Cut in butter or margarine. Stir in nuts.

Last-Minute Icing:
Mix all ingredients in a small bowl. Beat until smooth.

Caramel-Filled Danish

The new and different taste is from the yogurt.

2 pkgs. active dry yeast
1/2 cup warm water (110°F, 45°C)
4 cups all-purpose flour
1/2 cup sugar
1 teaspoon salt
1 cup cold butter or margarine,
   cut in small pieces

1 cup plain yogurt
2 eggs
1 teaspoon vanilla extract
Caramel Filling, see below
Sugar Glaze, see below

Caramel Filling:
1 cup light-brown sugar, firmly packed
1 cup chopped walnuts

1/2 teaspoon cinnamon

Sugar Glaze:
1 cup sifted powdered sugar
2 tablespoons milk

1/2 teaspoon vanilla extract

Lightly butter a large bowl to hold rising dough; set aside. In a small bowl, dissolve yeast in warm water. In another large bowl, mix flour, sugar and salt. With a pastry blender, cut in butter or margarine until mixture resembles cornmeal in texture. In another small bowl, stir yogurt until creamy. Blend in eggs, yeast mixture and vanilla extract. Stir into flour mixture. Mix well to form a soft dough. Place in buttered bowl. Turn dough to butter top. Cover and refrigerate overnight. Prepare Caramel Filling and set aside. Divide dough in half. Refrigerate half for future use. Grease 2 baking sheets. Set aside. On a lightly floured surface, roll out other half of dough to a 12" x 15" rectangle. Spread Caramel Filling evenly over dough, leaving 1/2-inch margin on all sides. Roll dough lengthwise like a jelly roll. Pinch edges and ends to seal. Cut rolled dough into 1-inch slices by placing a piece of strong thread crosswise under the roll. Cross the ends and pull thread through the dough. Place slices on prepared baking sheets. Cover and let rise in a warm place until almost doubled in bulk, about 30 minutes. Repeat with remaining dough. Preheat oven to 350°F (175°C). Bake about 20 minutes until golden brown. Prepare Sugar Glaze. Drizzle glaze over warm rolls. Makes about 36 rolls.

Caramel Filling:
In a small bowl, mix sugar, walnuts and cinnamon together.

Sugar Glaze:
In a small bowl, mix sugar, milk and vanilla together.

Cinnamon Bread Roll

If you don't have time before breakfast, make if for midmorning brunch.

5-1/2 to 6 cups all-purpose flour
2 pkgs. active dry yeast
1/2 teaspoon baking soda
1 cup plain yogurt, room temperature
3/4 cup water
1/4 cup sugar

1/3 cup butter or margarine
2 teaspoons salt
2 eggs
1 cup sugar
1 tablespoon cinnamon
2 tablespoons butter or margarine, melted

Generously grease two 9" x 5" loaf pans. In a large bowl, combine 2 cups flour, yeast and baking soda. In a 1-quart saucepan, stir yogurt until creamy. Add water, 1/4 cup sugar, 1/3 cup butter or margarine and salt. Cook over low heat until warm, 120°F (50°C). Butter or margarine does not need to melt. Add yogurt mixture to flour mixture. Beat at medium speed about 3 minutes until smooth. Blend in eggs. Gradually stir in enough remaining flour to make a moderately soft dough. On a lightly floured surface, knead dough about 5 minutes until smooth and elastic. Cover dough with wax paper and let stand 20 minutes. Combine 1 cup sugar and cinnamon in a small bowl. Set aside. Divide dough in half. Roll out each half to a 9" x 14" rectangle. Brush with 2 tablespoons melted butter or margarine. Sprinkle with half the cinnamon-sugar mixture. Beginning at end, roll dough tightly like a jelly roll. Pinch ends to seal. Fold ends under and place seam-side down in prepared pans. Cover and let rise in a warm place until doubled in bulk, about 45 minutes. Preheat oven to 375°F (190°C). Bake about 40 minutes until golden brown. Remove from pans immediately. Cool on wire racks. Makes 2 loaves.

How To Make Caramel-Filled Danish

1/Spread Caramel filling over half of dough, leaving 1/2-inch margin on all sides. Roll up jelly-roll fashion. Seal by pinching ends and edges with fingers.

2/Tie off dough into 1-inch slices, using strong thread. Place slices on greased baking sheets.

Raisin-Bran Muffins

A nutritional fun food.

3 cups bran flakes
1-1/4 cups all-purpose flour
1/2 cup sugar
1-1/4 teaspoons baking soda
1/4 teaspoon salt

1 cup plain yogurt, room temperature
1 egg, slightly beaten
1/4 cup vegetable oil or melted shortening
1/2 cup raisins

Preheat oven to 400°F (205°C). Grease muffin pans and set aside. In a large bowl, mix bran flakes, flour, sugar, baking soda and salt. In a small bowl, stir yogurt until creamy. Blend in egg. Drizzle oil or melted shortening into yogurt-egg mixture. Mix well. Stir yogurt mixture into bran flake mixture until flour mixture is just moistened. Fold in raisins. Fill prepared muffin cups 2/3 full. Bake 10 to 15 minutes until lightly browned. Remove from pan immediately. Serve warm. Makes 12 to 16 muffins.

Pear-Yogurt Muffins

Start your day with this delicate blend.

1 (16-oz.) can pears, drained
2 cups sifted all-purpose flour
1/2 cup sugar
1-1/2 teaspoons baking powder
1 teaspoon baking soda

1/2 teaspoon salt
1 cup plain yogurt, room temperature
1 egg, slightly beaten
1/4 cup vegetable oil or melted shortening
2 teaspoons grated lemon peel

Preheat oven to 400°F (205°C). Generously grease muffin pans. Set aside. Dice pears and set aside. In a large bowl, sift flour, sugar, baking powder, baking soda and salt. In a small bowl, stir yogurt until creamy. Blend in egg. Drizzle oil or melted shortening into yogurt-egg mixture, mixing well. Add lemon peel. Pour all at once into flour mixture. Gently fold in pears. Stir until flour mixture is just moistened. Fill prepared muffin cups 2/3 full. Bake 20 to 25 minutes until golden brown. Remove from pans immediately. Serve warm. Makes 12 to 16 muffins.

To reheat muffins, preheat the oven to 400°F (205°C). Wrap muffins in foil and heat in oven 15 to 20 minutes.

Creamy Oatmeal

A good way to start your day.

1-1/2 cups water
1/4 teaspoon salt
2/3 cup quick-cooking oats

1 teaspoon butter or margarine
1 tablespoon brown sugar
1/4 cup plain yogurt, room temperature

In a medium saucepan, bring water and salt to a boil. Stir in oats, butter or margarine and brown sugar. Cook 1 minute, stirring occasionally. Cover and remove from heat. Let stand a few minutes. Stir yogurt until creamy. Spoon 2 tablespoons yogurt over each serving. Serve immediately. Makes about 2 servings.

Fancy Farina

Dress up farina with fruit-flavored yogurt.

3 cups water
2 tablespoons butter
1 teaspoon salt

1/2 cup quick-cooking farina
1/4 cup fruit-flavored yogurt, room
   temperature

In a medium saucepan, bring water, butter and salt to a boil. Slowly add farina, stirring constantly. Bring to a second boil. Reduce heat and simmer 3 to 5 minutes, stirring constantly. Remove from heat. Stir yogurt until creamy. Slowly fold yogurt into farina. Serve immediately. Makes 4 servings.

Variation

Substitute honey-flavored yogurt for fruit-flavored yogurt.

Triple Treat Breakfast Cereal

Use your favorite cereals for variety.

2 cups cornflakes
2 cups wheat flakes
2 cups bran flakes

1 cup raisins
3 cups honey-flavored yogurt
1/3 cup slivered almonds, if desired

In a large bowl, mix cornflakes, wheat flakes, bran flakes and raisins. Stir yogurt until creamy. Place about 1 cup cereal mixture into 6 individual cereal bowls. Pour 1/2 cup yogurt over each serving. Garnish with slivered almonds, if desired. Makes 6 servings.

Continental Omelet

A superb brunch!

2 tablespoons butter or margarine
1/2 lb. chicken livers, cut in half
1/2 teaspoon salt
1/8 teaspoon white pepper
1/4 teaspoon oregano
3 eggs

1/2 teaspoon salt
1/8 teaspoon pepper
1 tablespoon butter or margarine
1/2 cup plain yogurt, room temperature
1 small tomato, peeled, seeded and chopped
1 tablespoon snipped chives

In a medium skillet, melt 2 tablespoons butter or margarine. Add chicken livers, 1/2 teaspoon salt, 1/8 teaspoon white pepper and oregano. Sauté chicken livers about 5 minutes. Cover and keep warm. In a small bowl, beat eggs, 1/2 teaspoon salt and 1/8 teaspoon pepper with a whisk. In a 9-inch omelet pan over medium heat, melt 1 tablespoon butter or margarine. Add egg mixture. Slide spatula around edge of pan, carefully lifting egg mixure so uncooked eggs will flow underneath. Cook until set. Carefully place on warm platter. Stir yogurt until creamy. Arrange cooked chicken livers and chopped tomato over top of omelet. Spoon yogurt on top. Sprinkle with chives. Makes 2 to 3 servings.

Variation

Substitute 1/2 pound cooked and crumbled bacon or sausage for chicken livers.

Blueberry Muffins

What could be better than homemade blueberry muffins?

2-1/2 cups all-purpose flour
3/4 cup sugar
2 teaspoons baking powder
1 teaspoon baking soda
1/2 teaspoon salt
1/2 cup butter or margarine

1 cup plain yogurt, room temperature
2 eggs, slightly beaten
1 teaspoon vanilla extract
1-1/2 cups fresh or thawed and drained
    frozen blueberries

Preheat oven to 400°F (205°C). Generously grease muffin pans. In a large bowl, mix flour, sugar, baking powder, baking soda and salt. With a pastry blender, cut in butter or margarine until mixture resembles fine crumbs. In a small bowl, stir yogurt until creamy. Blend in eggs and vanilla. Pour all at once into flour mixture. Stir until flour mixture is just moistened. Gently fold in blueberries. Fill prepared muffin cups 2/3 full. Bake 15 to 20 minutes until golden brown. Remove from pans immediately. Serve warm. Makes 12 to 16 muffins.

Fluffy Pancakes

The aroma of pancakes and hot coffee will rouse all the sleepy-heads.

1 egg	1 teaspoon baking powder
1 cup plain yogurt, room temperature	1/2 teaspoon baking soda
2 tablespoons vegetable oil	1/4 teaspoon salt
1 cup all-purpose flour	Melted butter
2 tablespoons sugar	Syrup

Preheat griddle to 375°F (190°C). In a medium bowl, beat egg until thick. Gradually add yogurt, beating constantly. Drizzle oil into egg-yogurt mixture, beating well. Add flour, sugar, baking powder, baking soda and salt. Beat well. Lightly oil hot griddle. Pour about 1/4 cup batter onto griddle. Turn when pancakes are puffy and covered with bubbles. Brown second side 1 to 2 minutes. Serve with melted butter and syrup. Makes about 10 pancakes.

Yogurt Crepes

These crepes are perfect with your favorite filling.

1 cup plain yogurt	1 cup all-purpose flour
1/2 cup water	1 tablespoon sugar
3 eggs, slightly beaten	1/8 teaspoon salt
2 tablespoons vegetable oil	Butter or margarine for frying

In a medium bowl, stir yogurt until creamy. Add water and eggs. Beat well. Drizzle oil into yogurt mixture. Stir in flour, sugar and salt. Use immediately or refrigerate for several hours. Brush an 8-inch crepe pan or skillet with butter or margarine. Place pan over medium-high heat until hot enough to sizzle a drop of water. For each crepe, pour 3 to 4 tablespoons batter into pan, rotating pan as batter is poured. Cook until lightly browned on bottom. Turn to brown other side, if desired. Brush crepe pan with more butter or margarine, if necessary. Stack crepes between paper towels or wax paper until ready to use. Fill warm crepes as desired. Makes about 14 crepes.

For special scrambled eggs, beat 2 eggs with 1 tablespoon yogurt. Scramble as usual.

Frittata

The classic omelet, Italian-style.

1 tablespoon butter or margarine	2 tablespoons chopped green pepper
1 teaspoon vegetable oil	2 tablespoons seeded and chopped tomato
2 eggs	Dash garlic powder
2 tablespoons plain yogurt	1 tablespoon grated Parmesan cheese
1/4 cup grated Romano cheese	Salt and pepper to taste
1 green onion, thinly sliced	

In a heavy skillet with a nonstick surface, heat butter or margarine and oil over medium heat. In a medium bowl, beat eggs. Add remaining ingredients. Mix well. Pour into center of preheated pan. Cook 3 to 5 minutes until all liquid is solidified and bottom of omelet is golden brown. Remove pan from heat; place a dinner plate over pan and flip omelet onto dinner plate. Makes 1 serving.

Variation

Grecian Omelet: Substitute 1/4 cup Greek feta cheese for 1/4 cup Romano cheese.

Ham Quiche Lorraine

Dieters can omit the pastry shell and enjoy this quiche with fewer calories.

1 9-inch pie shell, baked and cooled	2 teaspoons cornstarch
1 cup diced cooked ham	4 eggs
2 tablespoons butter or margarine	1/2 teaspoon salt
1 medium onion, chopped	1/4 teaspoon white pepper
6-oz. Swiss cheese, shredded	1/8 teaspoon nutmeg
1-1/2 cups plain yogurt, room temperature	

Preheat oven to 375°F (190°C). Sprinkle 3/4 cup of the diced ham in bottom of pastry shell. Thinly shred and mince remaining 1/4 cup ham for topping. In a small skillet melt butter or margarine. Sauté onion until golden. Remove and sprinkle over ham. Spread cheese evenly over ham and onion. In a medium bowl, stir yogurt and cornstarch until creamy. Add eggs, salt, white pepper and nutmeg. Beat to blend well. Pour over ham mixture. Sprinkle with remaining minced ham. Bake 35 to 40 minutes until a knife inserted near center comes out clean. Let stand 10 minutes before cutting. Makes about 6 servings.

Variation

Substitute 3/4 pound diced, cooked and drained bacon or 1 pound cooked and crumbled skinless pork sausage for the ham.

Cheese-Ham Roll-Ups

Here's a magical recipe with 3 secret ingredients!

1 (15-oz.) can whole asparagus spears
8 thin slices cooked ham
1/4 cup ginger ale
1 cup plain yogurt, room temperature

1 (1.25-oz.) pkg. cheese sauce mix
4 slices buttered toast, cut in half
Paprika, for garnish
Parsley, for garnish

Preheat oven to 400°F (205°C). Divide asparagus evenly into 8 portions. Roll each portion in a slice of ham. Put each ham roll-up seam-side down in an 11" x 7" baking dish. Brush with ginger ale. Bake 8 minutes until ham is cooked. In a 1-quart saucepan, stir yogurt until creamy. Blend in cheese sauce mix. Cook over low heat about 7 minutes, stirring constantly until thick. Place roll-ups on buttered toast slices. Pour hot sauce over and sprinkle with paprika. Garnish with parsley. Makes about 4 servings.

Spinach Soufflé Squares

You don't have to be a gourmet cook to make this.

1 tablespoon butter or margarine,
  softened
3 tablespoons grated Parmesan cheese
2 tablespoons butter or margarine
4 tablespoons flour
1 cup plain yogurt, room temperature
1/2 teaspoon salt
1/8 teaspoon white pepper

6 jumbo eggs, separated,
  room temperature
1/2 cup grated Parmesan cheese
1/2 cup crumbled feta cheese
1/4 teaspoon cream of tartar
1 (10-oz.) pkg. frozen chopped spinach,
  cooked and drained

Preheat oven to 350°F (175°C). Coat a 13" x 9" glass baking dish with 1 tablespoon soft butter or margarine. Sprinkle 3 tablespoons grated Parmesan cheese over bottom of baking dish. In a small saucepan, melt 2 tablespoons butter or margarine. Stir in flour. Cook over medium heat 2 to 3 minutes, being careful not to brown flour. Stir yogurt until creamy. Slowly blend into flour mixture. Add salt and white pepper. Cook until thick. Remove from heat. Beat egg yolks. Stir about 2 tablespoons hot yogurt mixture into beaten egg yolks. Mix well. Stir yolk mixture into sauce. Add 1/2 cup Parmesan cheese and all of feta cheese. Mix well. Cover and set aside. At this point the mixture may be stored in the refrigerator for several hours, then reheated over very low heat until lukewarm, stirring constantly. In a large bowl, beat egg whites until frothy. Add cream of tartar and beat until stiff but not dry. Do not overbeat. Stir about 1 cup of the egg whites into the lukewarm sauce. Fold in remaining whites with a rubber spatula. Carefully fold in cooked spinach. Pour into prepared dish and bake 20 to 25 minutes until a knife inserted in center comes out clean. Serve immediately. Makes 4 to 6 servings.

Appetizers & Beverages

An old proverb says that the beginning is half the undertaking. If your guests like the appetizers, they're sure to enjoy the rest of the dinner.

One of the secrets of being a good hostess is to serve the unusual. A few unique, perfectly prepared appetizers are better than a myriad of ordinary ones. This is where yogurt comes in. It adds zesty flavor to Apricot-Glazed Meatballs and Pizza-Rettas. Green Goddess Dip will whet everyone's appetite for your special main course. Serve Deviled Eggs and Easy Liver Pâté any afternoon.

Concerned about calories? Nibble to your heart's content on assorted crisp raw vegetable dippers served with Classic Yogurt Dip or Famous California Dip. Yogurt appetizers are low in calories but high in taste. Pull out your favorite appetizer recipes and replace part of the liquid, mayonnaise or sour cream with yogurt. You'll see and taste the difference!

Yogurt Cooler is a great thirst quencher on a hot summer day. Yogurt blends well with all fruit juice concentrates, tomato juice and nectars. Experiment with your favorite fruit drinks by replacing part of the liquid with plain or flavored yogurt.

SHAMROCK PARTY
Green Goddess Dip, page 35
Raw Vegetable Dippers
Cucumber Sandwiches, page 171
French-Dipped Tenderloin & Cocktail Buns
Green Relishes
Mints

FOOTBALL PREVIEW
Pizza-Rettas, page 33
Green Olive Dip
Ham Roll-Ups
Assorted Cheese
Cold Meat Platter
Mixed Nuts

FOURTH OF JULY SPARKLE
Chicken Drumsticks
Stuffed Mushroom Crowns
Nutty Cheese Log, page 163
Ruffled Chips & Crackers
Famous California Dip, page 37

DERBY PARTY
Apricot-Glazed Meatballs, page 32
Artichoke Appetizers, page 166
Cheddar Cheese Ball
Shrimp Dip
Assorted Crackers

Apricot-Glazed Meatballs

Get the party off to a delicious start with meatballs in tangy yogurt sauce.

Apricot Sauce, see below
5 slices dry white bread
Cold water
1-1/2 lbs. ground pork or beef
1 medium onion, minced
2 eggs, slightly beaten
3 tablespoons dry white wine

2 tablespoons minced parsley
1-1/2 teaspoons salt
1/4 teaspoon pepper
Dash allspice
Flour for dredging
Oil for frying

Apricot Sauce:
1 (12-oz.) jar apricot preserves
1 cup plus 2 tablespoons barbecue sauce

1/2 cup plain yogurt, room temperature

Prepare Apricot Sauce. Set aside. Soak bread slices in a little cold water. Squeeze lightly to remove excess water. Place ground meat in a large bowl. Add bread, onion, eggs, wine, parsley, salt, pepper and allspice. Mix. Shape mixture into 1/2-inch meatballs. Roll in flour. Heat oil in a large skillet. Add meatballs. Fry 20 to 25 minutes until evenly browned. Remove meatballs and drain excess fat. Put Apricot Sauce and meatballs in skillet. Cook over very low heat 30 minutes until browned. Serve warm. Makes about 60 meatballs.

Apricot Sauce:
In a medium saucepan, combine preserves and barbecue sauce. Heat until bubbly. Remove from heat. In a small bowl, stir yogurt until creamy. Slowly stir about 2 tablespoons hot sauce into yogurt. Carefully blend yogurt mixture into remaining sauce.

Easy Liver Pâté

Try it as a sandwich spread.

1/3 cup plain yogurt
1 (8-oz.) pkg. braunschweiger (liver sausage)
1 (4-oz.) can mushroom pieces and stems, drained
1 small onion, cut in half

2 tablespoons pickle relish
1 garlic clove
1/2 teaspoon salt
Assorted chips or crackers

Place yogurt and half the braunschweiger in a blender. Cover and blend on high speed 2 to 3 minutes until smooth. Add remaining braunschweiger, mushrooms, onion, pickle relish, garlic and salt. Continue to blend on high speed until smooth. Refrigerate about 2 hours before serving. Serve with chips or crackers. Makes about 3 cups.

Pizza-Rettas

A mini-pizza crescent made with yogurt dough—delicious and inexpensive.

1-1/4 cups sifted all-purpose flour,
   more if needed
1/4 teaspoon salt
1/3 cup plain yogurt

3 tablespoons butter or margarine, melted
Pizza Filling, see below
1 egg, slightly beaten

Pizza Filling:
1 lb. bulk Italian sausage
1 tablespoon minced onion
1/2 cup pizza sauce

1/4 teaspoon oregano
Few sprigs parsley, minced

Generously grease 2 baking sheets. In a medium bowl, sift together flour and salt. Stir in yogurt and butter or margarine. On a lightly floured surface, knead gently to form a smooth dough. Add more flour if needed. Cover dough with wax paper and let stand 30 minutes. Prepare Pizza Filling. Preheat oven to 400°F (205°C). Divide dough into thirds. Roll out each third to a 9-inch circle. Cut each circle into 8 wedges. Place a heaping teaspoon of Pizza Filling on the wide end of each wedge. Roll up each wedge from the wide end. Place point-side down in crescent shape on prepared baking sheets. Brush with egg. Prick tops with a fork. Bake in preheated oven about 10 to 12 minutes until golden brown. Makes 24 appetizers.

Pizza Filling:
In a medium skillet, cook sausage and onion about 10 minutes, stirring occasionally, until sausage is browned. Drain excess fat. Add pizza sauce, oregano and parsley. Cook about 5 minutes until heated through. Drain any remaining liquid. Cool.

Deviled Eggs

Devilishly good!

4 hard-cooked eggs
3 tablespoons plain yogurt
1 teaspoon prepared mustard
1/2 teaspoon horseradish

1/4 teaspoon salt
Few grains white pepper
Paprika, for garnish
Parsley sprigs, for garnish

Cut eggs in half lengthwise, using a knife to make scalloped edges. If desired, cut a thin slice off the bottom of each egg half so the halves will stand flat. Remove yolks. Place yolks in a small bowl and mash. Stir in yogurt. Add mustard, horseradish, salt and white pepper. Blend well. Spoon into egg halves. Sprinkle with paprika and garnish with sprigs of parsley. Makes 8 deviled eggs.

Green Goddess Dip

Divinely different!

1/2 cup cottage cheese
1 tablespoon anchovy paste
4 sprigs parsley
1 teaspoon Worcestershire sauce
1/2 teaspoon dry mustard

1 garlic glove, cut in half
1 tablespoon snipped chives
1 cup plain yogurt
Chips or assorted raw vegetable dippers

Place cottage cheese, anchovy paste, parsley, Worcestershire sauce, dry mustard, garlic and chives in a blender. Cover and blend on high speed 3 to 5 minutes until smooth. Stir in yogurt. Refrigerate about 2 hours before serving. Serve with chips or assorted raw vegetable dippers. Makes about 1-1/2 cups.

Aloha Fruit & Dip

An exotic dip for a Luau party.

10 small macaroons
1 pint plain yogurt
1/4 cup light brown sugar, firmly packed
1 large pineapple
Seedless green grapes

Sliced peaches
Sliced pears
Assorted berries
Kirsch liqueur

Place macaroons in a sturdy plastic bag. With a rolling pin, crush macaroons in small pieces. In a medium bowl, stir yogurt until creamy. Blend in brown sugar and macaroon pieces. Chill several hours to soften macaroon crumbs. Slice a cap-shaped piece off top of pineapple about 1 inch below bottom of leaves. With a sharp knife, hollow out center of pineapple, leaving a firm shell. Discard hard core. Reserve shell. Cut pineapple fruit into chunks. Fill shell with yogurt-macaroon dip. Place shell in center of a large platter. Replace pineapple cap if desired. Arrange pineapple chunks, grapes, peaches, pears and berries in groups around pineapple shell. Sprinkle fruit with kirsch liqueur. Serve immediately. Makes about 2-1/2 cups.

Yogurt Mock Puffs

Inspired by a famous Greek appetizer.

1 cup plain yogurt, cold
1 egg, slightly beaten
3-1/2 cups all-purpose flour
1 teaspoon salt
1/4 teaspoon baking soda

3 tablespoons vegetable oil
1 lb. butter or margarine,
   cut in 1/4-inch slices
Feta Cheese Filling, see below

Feta Cheese Filling:
3 eggs
1 lb. dry cottage cheese
1/2 lb. Greek feta cheese

1 teaspoon quick-cooking farina
Dash salt

In a large bowl, stir yogurt until creamy. Stir in egg. Add flour, salt, baking soda and oil. Mix until flour is moistened. Let stand 10 minutes. On a lightly floured surface, knead about 5 minutes until smooth. Add more flour if dough is sticky. Roll out to a 12" x 15" rectangle, keeping corners square. Spread butter or margarine over dough. Carefully fold 1/3 of dough toward center. Fold remaining third over 2 layers of dough and pinch edges together. Carefully fold the long rectangle again to form a square by folding 1/3 of dough toward center and remaining third of dough over 2 layers of dough. Pinch edges together. Wrap well in wax paper. Refrigerate 30 minutes. Unroll dough and repeat rolling, folding and chilling 2 more times. After last folding, rewrap tightly in wax paper. Refrigerate 5 hours or overnight. Prepare Feta Cheese Filling. Line baking sheets with wax paper. Divide chilled dough in half. Refrigerate half. Place other half on a lightly floured surface. Roll out to a 15" x 18" rectangle. Cut into 3-inch squares. Place about 1/2 teaspoon Feta Cheese Filling on each square. Fold opposite corner over filling, forming a triangle. Pinch edges together. Place on prepared baking sheets. At this point puffs may be frozen. If puffs are not to be frozen, refrigerate 30 minutes. Preheat oven to 350°F (175°C). Bake about 30 minutes until golden brown and puffy. Repeat with remaining dough. If puffs are frozen, place directly in preheated 350°F (175°C) oven and bake about 35 minutes until golden brown and puffy. Makes 60 puffs.

Feta Cheese Filling:
In a small bowl, beat eggs. Blend in cottage cheese, feta cheese, farina and salt. Mix well.

Try Thousand Island Dressing, page 51, as a fresh vegetable dip using carrot sticks, celery fans, mushrooms and cauliflowerets for dippers.

Guacamole

Olé! For your next fiesta.

3 ripe avocados
2 tablespoons grated onion
2 to 3 teaspoons chili powder
1/2 teaspoon salt
1 teaspoon vegetable oil

2 medium, ripe tomatoes, peeled, seeded and chopped
1 cup plain yogurt
1/2 teaspoon lemon juice
Tortilla chips or corn chips

Cut avocados in half lengthwise. Remove seeds and skin. Mash avocados in a medium bowl. Stir in onion, chili powder, salt, oil and tomatoes. Mix until smooth. Stir yogurt until creamy. Add to avocado mixture. Blend well. Sprinkle lemon juice on dip to prevent discoloring. Refrigerate about 2 hours before serving. Serve with tortilla chips or corn chips. Makes about 3 cups.

Famous California Dip

Terrific with vegetable dippers.

1 envelope onion soup mix
2 cups plain yogurt

Chips or crackers

In a small bowl, blend soup mix and yogurt. Refrigerate about 2 hours before serving. Serve with chips or crackers. Makes about 2 cups.

Red Riding Hood

My, what delightful drinks you serve!

3 cups tomato juice
1 cup plain yogurt
1 teaspoon Worcestershire sauce
1 teaspoon lemon juice

1 to 2 drops Tabasco® Sauce
Ice, if desired
4 celery sticks for garnish

Put tomato juice, yogurt, Worcestershire sauce, lemon juice and Tabasco® Sauce in a blender. Cover and blend on medium speed about 2 minutes until smooth. Pour into 4 tall glasses over ice, if desired. Place a celery stick in each glass for garnish. Serve immediately. Makes about 4 servings.

Classic Yogurt Dip

Watch your guests crowd around this one!

1 large cucumber
1 cup plain yogurt
1 tablespoon vegetable oil
1/8 teaspoon salt

1/8 teaspoon garlic powder
1/8 teaspoon dill weed
Sesame chips, crackers or assorted raw
   vegetable dippers

Peel cucumber. Cut in half and remove seeds. Grate enough cucumber to measure 1 cup. Drain well by pressing through a fine sieve. In a small bowl, stir yogurt until creamy. Drizzle oil into yogurt, stirring until smooth. Fold in drained cucumber, salt, garlic powder and dill weed. Refrigerate about 2 hours before serving. Serve with sesame chips, or assorted raw vegetable dippers. Makes about 1-1/2 cups.

How To Make Classic Yogurt Dip

1/Cut peeled cucumber in half and remove seeds with a spoon.

2/Drain grated cucumber well be pressing in a sieve before folding into yogurt.

Yogurt Milkshake

Packed with enough energy to make a light lunch.

1 cup plain yogurt
2 eggs
3 tablespoons honey

Dash salt
1 cup fresh or frozen strawberries,
   blueberries or raspberries

Put all ingredients in a blender. Cover and blend on high speed about 2 minutes until smooth and frothy. Pour into 2 tall glasses. Serve immediately. Makes about 2 servings.

Sunny Cooler

A frothy refresher that's delicious anytime.

1 cup plain yogurt
1/4 cup frozen orange juice concentrate

1 tablespoon sugar

Put yogurt, orange juice concentrate and sugar in a blender. Cover and blend on high speed about 2 minutes until smooth and frothy. Pour into a tall glass. Serve immediately. Makes about 1 serving.

Easy Eggnog

A honey of a drink.

1 cup vanilla-flavored yogurt
1 egg

2 tablespoons honey
Nutmeg

Put yogurt, egg and honey in a blender. Cover and blend on high speed about 2 minutes until smooth and frothy. Pour into a tall glass. Sprinkle with nutmeg. Serve immediately. Makes about 1 serving.

For a quick cooler, combine 1 cup yogurt, 1 tablespoon grape jelly and 12 ounces ginger ale in a blender. Cover and blend at high speed until frothy.

Mint Frappé

An after-dinner treat.

2 tablespoons crème de menthe
1 tablespoon white crème de cacao
1 cup Whipping Cream Yogurt, page 15,
   or plain yogurt

1 tablespoon powdered sugar

Put all ingredients in a blender. Cover and blend on high speed about 2 minutes until smooth and frothy. Pour into 2 tall glasses. Serve immediately. Makes about 2 servings.

Frosty Float

Tea lovers, try this.

3-1/2 cups milk
1 (6-oz.) can frozen orange juice concentrate,
   thawed

1/3 cup honey
1/3 cup instant tea powder
1 cup plain yogurt

Put milk, orange juice concentrate, honey, tea and yogurt in a blender. Cover and blend on high speed about 2 minutes until smooth and frothy. Pour into 6 tall glasses. Serve immediately. Makes about 6 servings.

Yogurt Cooler

A traditional Mediterranean thirst quencher.

1 cup plain yogurt
3 cups ice water

Dash salt, if desired

In a pitcher, beat together yogurt and water. Or put in a blender, cover and blend on high speed about 2 minutes until frothy. Pour into 4 tall glasses. Serve immediately or refrigerate. If refrigerated, stir before serving. Season with a dash of salt, if desired. Makes about 4 servings.

Peach Velvet

Nectar of the gods.

1 (12-oz.) can peach nectar
1 cup peach-flavored yogurt

2 tablespoons peach preserves
Freshly grated nutmeg

Put peach nectar, yogurt and peach preserves in a blender. Cover and blend on high speed about 2 minutes until smooth. Pour into 2 tall glasses. Sprinkle with freshly grated nutmeg. Serve immediately. Makes about 2 servings.

How To Make Peach Velvet

1/Place peach nectar, yogurt and preserves in the order given in a blender container. Cover and blend until smooth.

2/Grate nutmeg over the drink before serving.

Salads & Salad Dressings

Salads should be crisp, cool, colorful and always served on a chilled plate. The success of a salad depends on the dressing. It should enhance the salad's flavor and still keep its own character.

Dinner salads should be light and served with a tart dressing. Best-Ever Yogurt Dressing and Herb Salad Dressing are perfect with vegetable salads. Their tartness rounds out a fish main course better than a bland dressing. For poultry dinners, Sesame Seed Dressing served over fresh fruit is absolutely superb.

Traditional salads like Waldorf Salad, Creamy Potato Salad and Three-Bean Salad take on a new taste with yogurt. Try low-calorie yogurt in place of mayonnaise or sour cream in your favorite dressing. Measure the desired amount of yogurt and stir it with a wire whisk until it's creamy. Then blend in the other ingredients. Garden Salad Yogurt and Cucumber Yogurt, page 18, can also be used as a base for salad dressings.

Use plain or flavored yogurt for part of the liquid in your vegetable or fruit glasses. Lavish praises are in store when you place Frosty Fruit Mold on your dinner table.

ANNIVERSARY CELEBRATION
Appetizer Tray
Standing Rib Roast of Beef
Au Jus Gravy
Herb-Stuffed Baked Potatoes, page 100
Broccoli Parmesan
Frosty-Fruit Mold, page 44
Baked Alaska Flambé, page 139

SUNDAY SPECIAL
Roast Chicken
Oven Browned Potatoes
Waldorf Salad, page 43
Asparagus Spears
Chocolate Fudge Cake

BACKYARD BUFFET
Charcoal-Grilled Hamburgers
Three-Bean Salad, page 50
Corn on the Cob
Cabbage-Carrot Slaw, page 46
Potato Chips
Fudge Brownies

Waldorf Salad

Especially good with chicken.

2 sweet apples, cored and diced
2 pears, cored and diced
1/2 cup seedless grapes, cut in half
1/4 cup diced celery
1/4 cup coarsely chopped walnuts

1/4 cup chopped dates
1/2 cup plain yogurt
1 tablespoon powdered sugar
Lettuce cups
Paprika, for garnish

In a large bowl, toss apples, pears, grapes, celery, walnuts and dates. Blend yogurt and powdered sugar together. Pour over salad, toss lightly. Serve in lettuce cups. Sprinkle with paprika. Makes 4 servings.

Variation

Substitute 1/2 cup honey-flavored yogurt for 1/2 cup plain yogurt and 1 tablespoon powdered sugar.

How To Make Waldorf Salad

1/Dice apples, pears and celery before tossing. Halve grapes and chop walnuts and dates.

2/Gently toss ingredients to coat with yogurt and powdered sugar mixture before serving on a bed of crisp lettuce.

Frosty Fruit Mold

A refreshing fruit gelatin and yogurt medley.

1 (3-oz.) pkg. peach-flavored gelatin
1 cup boiling water

1 cup peach-flavored yogurt or plain yogurt
Orange Layer, see below

Orange Layer:
1 (3-oz.) pkg. orange-flavored gelatin
1 cup boiling water
1 cup orange-flavored yogurt

1 (11-oz.) can mandarin orange sections,
   drained well

Generously oil a 6-cup mold. Set aside. In a medium bowl, dissolve peach-flavored gelatin in boiling water. Refrigerate 10 minutes to cool slightly. Stir peach-flavored or plain yogurt until creamy. With a whisk, blend into cooled gelatin mixture. Chill to consistency of unbeaten egg white. Beat with an electric mixer on low speed until frothy. Pour into prepared mold. Refrigerate about 2 hours until completely set. Prepare Orange Layer. Spoon into mold over set first layer. Refrigerate 4 hours. Makes about 8 servings.

Orange Layer:
In a medium bowl, dissolve orange-flavored gelatin in boiling water. Refrigerate 10 minutes to cool slightly. Stir orange-flavored yogurt until creamy. With a whisk, blend into cooled gelatin mixture. Chill to consistency of unbeaten egg white. Fold in mandarin orange sections.

Ambrosia

A delectable salad or satisfying dessert.

1 (1-lb. 4-oz.) can pineapple chunks,
   drained well
1 (11-oz.) can mandarin oranges,
   drained well

1/2 cup flaked coconut
1 cup plain yogurt

In a medium bowl, lightly toss pineapple chunks, mandarin oranges and coconut. Stir yogurt until creamy. Add to pineapple-orange mixture. Gently fold in yogurt until fruit is coated. Serve immediately. Makes about 4 servings.

Cabbage-Carrot Slaw

Colorful cole slaw with superb flavor.

Creamy Dressing, see below
3 cups shredded cabbage

1 (4-oz.) can crushed pineapple, drained
2 carrots, shredded

Creamy Dressing:
1 cup plain yogurt
2 tablespoons sugar
1/4 teaspoon celery seed

1 teaspoon salt
1 tablespoon vinegar

Prepare Creamy Dressing. In a large bowl, toss cabbage, crushed pineapple and carrots. Pour dressing over all and toss to coat well. Refrigerate 1 hour before serving. Makes about 6 servings.

Creamy Dressing:
In a small bowl, stir yogurt until creamy. Add remaining ingredients. Blend well.

Low-Cal Slaw

Great for the waistline, too!

Celery Seed Dressing, see below
3 cups shredded cabbage

1 small onion, chopped
1 small carrot, grated

Celery Seed Dressing:
1/2 cup plain yogurt
1 tablespoon vegetable oil
1-1/2 tablespoons vinegar
2 tablespoons sugar

1/2 teaspoon salt
3/4 teaspoon celery seed
1/4 teaspoon dry mustard

Prepare Celery Seed Dressing. In a large bowl, toss shredded cabbage, onion and carrot. Pour Celery Seed Dressing over salad and toss well. Makes about 6 servings.

Celery Seed Dressing:
In a small bowl, stir yogurt until creamy. Drizzle oil into yogurt, stirring constantly. Add vinegar. Stir in remaining ingredients and beat slightly.

Wholesome Vegetable Salad

Attractive surroundings for your favorite raw vegetables.

1 envelope plus 1 teaspoon unflavored
   gelatin
1/4 cup cold water
1/2 cup boiling water
1/2 cup sugar
3/4 teaspoon salt
2 tablespoons white vinegar
1 cup lemon-flavored yogurt

3/4 cup shredded cabbage
1/3 cup diced green pepper
1/2 cup chopped celery
1/3 cup shredded carrot
1/4 cup sliced pimiento-stuffed olives
2 tablespoons minced onion
Lettuce cups

Generously oil a 4-cup mold or 6 individual molds. Soften gelatin in cold water. Add boiling water and stir to dissolve gelatin. Add sugar, salt and vinegar. Stir until sugar is dissolved. Stir yogurt until creamy. With a whisk, blend yogurt into gelatin mixture. Refrigerate until slightly thickened. Stir in cabbage, green pepper, celery, carrot, olives and onion. Pour into prepared mold. Refrigerate about 4 hours until firm. Serve in lettuce cups. Makes about 6 servings.

Dill-Dressed Tomatoes

A dynamic way to serve tomatoes.

1/2 cup plain yogurt
1 tablespoon mayonnaise or mayonnaise-style
   salad dressing
1/4 teaspoon dill weed
1-1/2 teaspoons lemon juice

1/8 teaspoon dry mustard
Dash cayenne pepper
Dash salt
3 large tomatoes

In a small bowl, stir yogurt until creamy. Stir in mayonnaise or salad dressing, dill weed, lemon juice, dry mustard, cayenne pepper and salt. Refrigerate about 1 hour. Peel and slice tomatoes. Place in a shallow bowl. Pour dressing over tomatoes. Makes about 6 servings.

For a quick salad dressing over a fruit salad, stir 1 cup fruit yogurt and pour over salad. Sprinkle with chopped nuts.

Garden Fresh Mold

Crisp, spring garden flavors.

2 (3-oz.) pkgs. lime-flavored gelatin
2 tablespoons unflavored gelatin
3 cups boiling water
1 tablespoon vinegar
2 teaspoons salt
2 cups plain yogurt

1 cup grated cucumber, drained
1 cup grated radishes, drained
1 cup finely minced green onions
Curly endive, for garnish
Radish roses, for garnish

Generously oil a 9-inch square pan or a 6-1/2-cup ring mold. In a large bowl, mix lime-flavored and unflavored gelatins. Add boiling water and stir to dissolve gelatin. Add vinegar and salt. Refrigerate until slightly thickened. With an electric mixer on low speed, beat gelatin mixture until frothy. Stir yogurt until creamy. Add to gelatin mixture. Beat well. Fold in cucumber, radishes and onions. Pour into prepared mold. Refrigerate about 4 hours until firm. Invert to unmold. Garnish with endive and radish roses. Makes 8 to 10 servings.

How To Make Garden Fresh Mold

1/Using an electric mixer, beat gelatin mixture until frothy. Add yogurt and beat to blend well.

2/With a spatula, fold in grated cucumbers, radishes and minced onions.

Rice Jumble Salad

An unusual salad that's sure to please.

Tangy Yogurt Dressing, see below
3 cups cooked rice, cooled
2 green peppers, chopped
2 medium tomatoes, peeled, seeded
   and cubed

2 pimientos, drained and chopped
2 small green onions, chopped
2 tablespoons minced parsley
Large lettuce leaves

Tangy Yogurt Dressing:
1/2 cup plain yogurt
1/4 cup vegetable oil
1 teaspoon salt

1 teaspoon vinegar
1/4 teaspoon white pepper
1 garlic clove, pressed

Prepare Tangy Yogurt Dressing. In a large bowl, gently toss rice, green peppers, tomatoes, pimientos, onions and parsley. Pour Tangy Yogurt Dressing over salad. Toss gently to mix. Chill before serving. Line serving dish with lettuce leaves. Spoon in salad. Makes about 8 servings.

Tangy Yogurt Dressing:
In a small bowl, stir yogurt until creamy. Drizzle oil into yogurt, stirring constantly. Add remaining ingredients. Blend well.

Herbed Potato Salad

The secret herb is powdered oregano.

2 lbs. potatoes
Water
1 teaspoon salt
1/2 cup plain yogurt
2 tablespoons vegetable oil
1 medium onion, chopped

2 tablespoons minced parsley
2 teaspoons vinegar
1/4 teaspoon powdered oregano
1/4 teaspoon salt
1/8 teaspoon white pepper
Paprika, for garnish

Cook potatoes in boiling water with 1 teaspoon salt. Drain. Peel potatoes and slice lengthwise. Place in a large bowl. In a small bowl, stir yogurt until creamy. Drizzle oil into yogurt, stirring constantly. Blend in onion, parsley, vinegar, oregano, 1/4 teaspoon salt and white pepper. Mix well. Pour over potatoes. Toss gently to coat well. Put in a serving bowl. Sprinkle with paprika. Serve immediately. Makes about 6 servings.

Creamy Potato Salad

Potatoes will peel much easier after cooking.

About 6 large potatoes
Water
1 teaspoon salt
4 hard-cooked eggs, chopped
1-1/2 cups chopped celery
1/2 green pepper, chopped
1 medium onion, chopped

1-1/2 cups plain yogurt
1 tablespoon vegetable oil
1 teaspoon salt
1-1/2 teaspoons prepared mustard
1/4 teaspoon white pepper
Paprika, for garnish
Parsley, for garnish

Cook unpeeled potatoes in boiling water with 1 teaspoon salt. Peel and dice enough to measure 4 cups. In a large bowl, gently toss potatoes, eggs, celery, green pepper and onion. In a small bowl, stir yogurt until creamy. Slowly drizzle oil into yogurt, stirring constantly. Blend in 1 teaspoon salt, mustard and white pepper. Gently fold into potato mixture. Sprinkle with paprika. Garnish with parsley. Makes about 8 servings.

Three-Bean Salad

Yogurt dressing makes tasty bean salad even better!

1 (16-oz.) can green beans, drained
1 (16-oz.) can yellow beans, drained
1 (1-lb. 5-oz.) can red kidney beans, drained
1/2 cup minced green pepper
1/2 cup minced celery
1 small onion, minced

1 (2-oz.) jar pimientos, drained and chopped
2/3 cup plain yogurt
1/3 cup vegetable oil
3/4 cup sugar
1 teaspoon salt
1 teaspoon pepper

In a large bowl, mix beans, green pepper, celery, onion and pimientos. In a small bowl, stir yogurt until creamy. Drizzle oil into yogurt, stirring constantly. Add sugar, salt and pepper. Stir until sugar is dissolved. Pour over bean mixture. Toss gently. Refrigerate several hours or overnight. Drain before serving. Makes about 8 to 10 servings.

Unless recipes call for ground herbs, crush dried herb leaves to release their full flavor.

Kidney Bean Salad

Take this along on your next picnic.

2 (1-lb.) cans red kidney beans, drained
1 cup chopped celery
1 small onion, chopped
1/2 cup chopped sweet pickles
2 hard-cooked eggs, chopped

1 teaspoon salt
1/2 cup plain yogurt
2 tablespoons mayonnaise-style salad
   dressing (not mayonnaise)

In a large bowl, toss beans, celery, onion, pickles, eggs and salt. In a small bowl, stir yogurt until creamy. Blend in salad dressing. Add yogurt mixture to bean mixture. Toss lightly. Makes about 4 to 6 servings.

Blue Cheese Dressing

Extra thick and creamy.

1 cup plain yogurt
2-1/2 oz. crumbled blue cheese
2 teaspoons grated onion
1 teaspoon vinegar

1/4 teaspoon sugar
1/4 teaspoon salt
Dash pepper

In a small bowl, stir yogurt until creamy. Blend in blue cheese, onion, vinegar, sugar, salt and pepper. Refrigerate about 2 hours in an airtight jar before serving. Makes about 1 cup.

Thousand Island Dressing

Serve this updated version over crisp fresh lettuce.

1 cup plain yogurt
2 tablespoons chili sauce
1 hard-cooked egg, chopped

2 tablespoons pickle relish
2 tablespoons mayonnaise
1 teaspoon sugar

Combine all ingredients in a small bowl. Blend well. Refrigerate about 2 hours in an airtight jar before serving. Makes about 1-1/2 cups.

Sesame Seed Dressing

For a truly natural treat, serve over fresh fruit salad.

3 tablespoons sesame seeds
1 cup honey-flavored yogurt

1 teaspoon grated orange peel

Preheat oven to 350°F (175°C). Put sesame seeds in a shallow baking pan. Toast 3 to 4 minutes. Cool slightly. In a small bowl, stir yogurt until creamy. Stir in sesame seeds and orange peel. Refrigerate about 2 hours in an airtight jar before serving. Makes about 1 cup.

Herb Salad Dressing

Your tossed green salad needs this!

1 cup plain yogurt
1/4 cup vegetable oil
2 tablespoons white vinegar
1/2 teaspoon oregano

1/2 teaspoon dill weed
1 teaspoon garlic salt
Dash pepper

In a small bowl, stir yogurt until creamy. Drizzle oil into yogurt, stirring until smooth. Stir in vinegar, oregano, dill weed, garlic salt and pepper. Blend well. Refrigerate about 2 hours in an airtight jar before serving. Makes about 1-1/3 cups.

Best-Ever Yogurt Dressing

The perfect dressing for your best tossed vegetable salad!

1 cup plain yogurt
3 tablespoons vegetable oil
1 tablespoon tarragon white wine vinegar
2 teaspoons chopped parsley
2 tablespoons grated onion

1/8 teaspoon ground oregano
1/2 teaspoon salt
1/4 teaspoon garlic powder
1/8 teaspoon white pepper

Put yogurt, oil, vinegar, parsley, onion, oregano, salt, garlic powder and white pepper in a blender. Cover and blend on high speed about 2 minutes until smooth and creamy. Refrigerate about 2 hours in an airtight jar before serving. Makes about 1-1/2 cups.

Soups & Sandwiches

Soups have always been popular in my family. My mother served soup with every meal. I updated my favorites for this book. Yogurt gives soup a distinctive touch. Swiss Chard Soup and Barley Soup have a delicate taste and are high in nutrition. Hungry Man's Borscht and Grandma's Vegetable Soup are hearty satisfying main courses served with crusty butter rolls and a crisp salad.

Yogurt should be at room temperature when added to soups. Always blend a little of the hot soup into the yogurt first to prevent curdling. If the recipe calls for 1/2 cup of yogurt, blend 2 tablespoons of hot soup into the yogurt. If 1 cup of yogurt is called for, blend about 1/4 cup of hot soup into the yogurt. Then gradually stir the yogurt-soup mixture into the remaining soup. If you don't plan to serve the entire pot of soup,

freeze or refrigerate the extra, and add yogurt only to the amount of soup you need. Yogurt is sensitive to high temperatures and will curdle if reheated. Curdling will not affect the taste of the soup. When you reheat the soup, stir in the yogurt just before serving, following the directions above.

If you need an impromptu soup, try yogurt with canned or dehydrated soups. Flavor it with herbs, cubed meat or chopped vegetables. Start with hot Creamy Potato Soup or cold Jiffy Tomato Soup and go on from there.

A sandwich should be custom-made to each person's taste. Take your pick from the unusual Super Gyros or Rye Pocket Reubens to Grilled Ham & Cheese Sandwiches. My son had a group of friends over and the Coney Island Dogs disappeared as fast as I could make them!

A DAY IN ATHENS
Super Gyros, page 67
Tossed Green Salad
With Black Olives & Feta Cheese
Oil & Vinegar Dressing
Walnut Cake
Honey Topping
Greek Coffee

INTERNATIONAL LUNCH
French Onion Soup
Rye Pocket Reubens, page 62
Fresh Fruit & Cheese Platter

FIESTA TOUCH
Gazpacho, page 59
Zucchini Tostadas, page 66
Avocado Salad
Mexican Wedding Cakes

DIETER'S LUNCH
Cottage Cucumber Soup, page 56
Tuna Salad in Lettuce Cups
Carrot Curls
Bread Sticks
Coffee or Tea

Garden Vegetable Soup

A cold soup that's low in calories and high in nutrition.

2 cups plain yogurt
1/2 cup cold water
1 teaspoon salt
1/2 teaspoon dill weed
1/8 teaspoon garlic powder
Dash white pepper

2 cups peeled, seeded and diced cucumber
1/2 cup diced radishes
2 green onions, thinly sliced
1/2 cup shredded lettuce
1/2 cup diced zucchini
2 tablespoons snipped parsley

In a large bowl, stir yogurt until creamy. Blend in water, salt, dill weed, garlic powder and white pepper. Add remaining ingredients. Mix well. Refrigerate about 1 hour before serving. Makes about 6 servings.

Split-Pea Soup

Herbs make this an exceptional soup.

1/2 lb. pkg. green split peas
1 ham bone
4 cups cold water
1 small bay leaf
1/4 cup diced carrot
1/4 cup minced onion
1/4 cup diced celery

1 small potato, diced
1/2 teaspoon salt
1/8 teaspoon crushed thyme leaves
2 sprigs parsley, chopped
Salt to taste
Freshly ground pepper to taste
2/3 cup plain yogurt, room temperature

Wash, rinse and sort peas. Put in a Dutch oven or heavy pot. Add ham bone, cold water, bay leaf, carrot, onion, celery, potato, 1/2 teaspoon salt and thyme. Bring to a boil. Cover and simmer about 1-1/2 hours. Remove bay leaf and ham bone. Puree soup by pressing it through a sieve or blending it in a blender on high speed about 3 minutes. Add more salt and freshly ground pepper to taste. In a small bowl, stir yogurt until creamy. Stir a small amount of soup into yogurt. Gradually add yogurt-soup mixture to remaining soup. Keep warm over very low heat. Do not boil. Makes 4 to 6 servings.

Garden Vegetable Soup and Sandwich Siciliana, page 61

Jiffy Tomato Soup

A quick and easy cold soup.

2 cups plain yogurt
1 (10-3/4-oz.) can condensed tomato soup,
  chilled
1/2 cup cold water

1 tablespoon snipped chives
1/2 teaspoon garlic salt
1/8 teaspoon pepper

In a medium bowl, stir yogurt until creamy. Blend in cold soup, cold water, chives, garlic salt and pepper. Mix well. Serve immediately or refrigerate until ready to serve. Makes about 4 servings.

Quick Hominy Soup

You'll be surprised how much you like this soup.

1 tablespoon butter
2 tablespoons minced onion
1 tablespoon flour
1 cup water

1 (20-oz.) can hominy
1/2 cup plain yogurt, room temperature
1 tablespoon brown sugar

Put butter, onion and flour in a 1-quart saucepan. Sauté until onion is golden. Stir in water and hominy. Bring to a boil. Simmer 7 minutes. Remove from heat. In a small bowl, stir yogurt until creamy. Stir a small amount of soup into yogurt. Gradually add yogurt-soup mixture to remaining soup. Sprinkle individual servings with brown sugar. Makes about 4 servings.

Cottage Cucumber Soup

My dieting friends enjoy this at snack time.

2 cups plain yogurt
1 cup small-curd cottage cheese
2 cups peeled, seeded and cubed cucumbers
1/4 teaspoon dill weed

1/2 teaspoon salt
Dash white pepper
Parsley sprigs, for garnish

Put yogurt and cottage cheese in a blender. Cover and blend on high speed about 2 minutes until smooth. Add cucumbers, dill weed, salt and white pepper. Cover and blend on high speed 2 to 3 minutes until creamy and smooth. Refrigerate about 1 hour before serving. Garnish each bowl with a parsley sprig. Makes about 4 servings.

Swiss Chard Soup

Prepare this soup the day before, then serve it hot or chilled.

1 lb. Swiss chard	1/4 cup quick-cooking barley
2 cups boiling water	6 cups water
3 tablespoons vegetable oil	1 cup plain yogurt, room temperature
1 medium onion, chopped	

Wash and drain Swiss chard. Slice finely. Blanch 2 minutes in 2 cups boiling water. Drain. Heat oil in a 3-quart saucepan. Add onion and sauté until golden. Add Swiss chard, barley and 6 cups water. Bring to a boil. Cover and simmer 30 minutes. Let stand 5 minutes or refrigerate until ready to serve. In a small bowl, stir yogurt until creamy. For cold soup, stir yogurt into soup. For hot soup, stir a small amount of hot soup into yogurt. Gradually add yogurt-soup mixture to remaining soup. Makes about 6 servings.

Creamy Potato Soup

Delicious with fish.

1 tablespoon butter or margarine	1/2 cup water
2 small green onions, thinly sliced	1/4 cup shredded Cheddar cheese
1/8 teaspoon white pepper	1/2 cup plain yogurt, room temperature
1 (10-1/2-oz.) can condensed cream of	
potato soup	

Melt butter or margarine in a medium saucepan. Sauté onions until soft. Stir in white pepper, cream of potato soup, water and cheese. Heat 5 to 7 minutes, stirring constantly, until mixture begins to bubble and cheese melts. In a small bowl, stir yogurt until creamy. Gradually stir into soup. Serve immediately. Makes about 2 servings.

Use plain yogurt to replace part of the water or milk in making canned soups.

Meatball Soup

Tangy and good.

1 lb. lean ground beef	Dash garlic powder
1 medium onion, chopped	1/8 teaspoon dill weed
1/2 cup uncooked rice	5 cups water
1 egg, slightly beaten	2 beef bouillon cubes
1/4 cup minced parsley	1 tablespoon butter or margarine
1/2 teaspoon salt	2 egg yolks
1/4 teaspoon pepper	1 cup plain yogurt, room temperature
1/8 teaspoon oregano	Lemon wedges, if desired

In a large bowl, lightly mix beef, onion, rice, 1 egg, parsley, salt, pepper, oregano, garlic powder and dill weed. Shape into 1-inch balls. Put water, bouillon cubes and butter or margarine in a large saucepan. Bring to a boil. Add meatballs to boiling broth. Cover and cook about 45 minutes. In a small bowl, beat egg yolks until thick. In another small bowl, stir yogurt until creamy. Gradually add to beaten yolks. Stir a small amount of hot broth into egg-yogurt mixture. Gradually stir egg-yogurt mixture into remaining broth. Serve immediately with lemon wedges, if desired. Makes about 6 servings.

Variation
Add 1 (1-lb.) can mixed vegetables to soup during last 5 minutes of cooking.

Barley Soup

A delectable soup—hot or cold.

2 tablespoons butter or margarine	1 cup quick-cooking barley
1 teaspoon dried mint leaves, crushed	2 teaspoons salt
2 quarts water	1 cup plain yogurt, room temperature

Melt butter or margarine in a Dutch oven or heavy pot. Add mint leaves and sauté about 15 seconds to coat mint leaves. Add water. Bring to a boil over high heat. Add barley and salt. Cover and reduce heat. Cook about 15 minutes until tender. Let stand 10 minutes. In a small bowl, stir yogurt until creamy. Stir a small amount of soup into yogurt. Gradually add yogurt-soup mixture to remaining soup. Keep warm over low heat. To serve cold, refrigerate several hours before serving. To reheat soup, cook over low heat about 10 minutes, stirring constantly. Makes about 8 servings.

Grandma's Vegetable Soup

The aroma brings back childhood memories.

8 cups beef broth
3 cups chopped celery
1 large onion, chopped
1 cup sliced carrots
1 green pepper, chopped
1/2 cup quick-cooking barley

1 (16-oz.) can tomato puree
1 tablespoon salt
1 teaspoon black pepper
1-1/2 cups cooked beef, cubed
1-1/2 cups plain yogurt, room temperature

In a large kettle, combine broth, celery, onion, carrots, green pepper, barley, tomato puree, salt and pepper. Bring to a boil. Cover and simmer 25 minutes. Add meat. Cook 10 more minutes. Remove from heat. In a small bowl, stir yogurt until creamy. Stir a small amount of hot soup into yogurt. Gradually add yogurt-soup mixture to remaining soup. Serve immediately. If you are not going to use all the soup, add yogurt only to what you plan to use. Stir in 1/2 cup yogurt per quart. Refrigerate or freeze remaining soup. Just before serving, heat soup and add yogurt according to directions above. Makes about 3 quarts, enough for 12 main dish servings.

Gazpacho

A delightful version of the popular cold Spanish soup.

1 (12-oz.) can tomato juice
1 cup plain yogurt
3 medium tomatoes, peeled
1 large cucumber, peeled and cubed
1 medium onion, halved
1 green pepper, quartered
2 cups chopped celery
1 small garlic clove

3 tablespoons vegetable oil
2 tablespoons red wine vinegar
1-1/2 teaspoons salt
Freshly ground pepper
5 drops Tabasco® sauce
Minced parsley, for garnish
Croutons, for garnish

Put tomato juice, yogurt, tomatoes, 1/2 the cucumber, 1/2 the onion, 1/2 the green pepper, celery and garlic in a blender. Cover and blend on high speed about 1 minute to puree vegetables. Mince remaining cucumber, onion and green pepper; chill in separate serving bowls. In a large bowl, pour in pureed vegetables. Drizzle oil into puree, stirring constantly. Blend in vinegar, salt, pepper and Tabasco® sauce. Cover. Refrigerate 3 to 4 hours. Chill serving bowls and soup tureen before serving. To serve, pour soup into chilled tureen. Sprinkle with minced parsley. Serve on a tray with reserved chopped vegetables and croutons for garnish. Makes about 6 servings.

Hungry Man's Borscht

A main-dish beef soup loaded with flavor.

2 quarts water
3 lbs. beef shinbone
1 lb. chuck roast
1 small bay leaf
4 teaspoons salt
1/4 teaspoon pepper
1 (8-oz.) can tomato sauce
2 tablespoons minced parsley

2 cups chopped celery
3 raw beets, diced
1 large onion, chopped
1 carrot, sliced
1 garlic clove, minced
1/2 medium cabbage, shredded
1-1/2 cups plain yogurt, room temperature

In a Dutch oven or large pot, pour water over shinbones and chuck roast. Add bay leaf, salt and pepper. Cover and simmer 1-1/2 hours. Remove shinbone and meat. Remove meat from bones. Dice all meat. Strain broth and return to pot. Add diced meat and remaining ingredients except yogurt. Simmer about 30 minutes until meat is tender and vegetables are cooked. Remove from heat. Let stand 15 minutes. In a small bowl, stir yogurt until creamy. Stir a small amount of hot soup into yogurt. Gradually add yogurt-soup mixture to remaining soup. Serve immediately. If you are not going to use all the soup, add yogurt only to what you plan to use. Stir in 1/2 cup yogurt per quart. Refrigerate or freeze remaining soup. Just before serving, heat soup and add yogurt according to directions above. Makes about 3 quarts, enough for 12 main dish servings.

Cold Potato Soup

A refreshing soup.

3 cups peeled and diced potatoes
2 cups cold water
1 teaspoon salt
2 cups plain yogurt
1/2 cup cold water

1 onion, minced
Dash white pepper
Salt to taste
Snipped chives, for garnish

Put diced potatoes, 2 cups water and 1 teaspoon salt in a medium saucepan. Cover and bring to a boil. Cook about 5 minutes until potatoes are soft. Drain. Refrigerate about 1 hour. In a soup tureen, stir yogurt until creamy. Add 1/2 cup water. Fold in potatoes, onion and white pepper. Add additional salt to taste. Refrigerate about 1 hour before serving. Sprinkle with chives. Makes about 4 servings.

Grilled Ham & Cheese Sandwiches

Family's supper or teenager's snack—everybody loves them.

1 tablespoon butter or margarine	8 thin slices Swiss cheese
3/4 cup chopped fresh mushrooms	8 thin slices cooked ham
1/3 cup thinly sliced green onions	8 slices white or whole-wheat bread
1/8 teaspoon salt	1 egg
Dash pepper	1/4 cup milk
3 tablespoons plain yogurt	Butter or margarine for frying

Preheat griddle to 350°F (175°C). Melt 1 tablespoon butter or margarine in a small skillet, add mushrooms and green onions. Sauté about 3 minutes. Remove from heat. Add salt and pepper. Stir in yogurt. Place a slice of cheese and a slice of ham on each of 4 slices of bread. Spoon about one-fourth of the mushroom mixture over the 4 sandwich halves. Top with remaining ham, cheese and bread. Lightly press edges together. In a pie plate, beat egg and milk together. Dip both sides of sandwiches into egg mixture. Brush preheated griddle with butter or margarine. Cook sandwiches on griddle 1 minute on each side or until golden brown. Serve immediately. Makes 4 sandwiches.

Sandwich Siciliana

Yogurt does wonders for Italian sausage.

4 Italian sausages	1 medium onion, chopped
3 tablespoons water	1 cup plain yogurt
2 tablespoons vegetable oil	4 small French rolls
1 large green pepper, cut in strips	Water

Preheat oven to 350°F (175°C). Place sausages and water in a medium skillet. Cover and cook about 15 minutes. Cook sausages uncovered about 15 more minutes until browned. Remove from skillet. Heat oil in skillet. Sauté green pepper and onion until onion is golden brown. Sprinkle French rolls with water. Wrap in foil and heat in oven 10 minutes. Put sautéed onion and green pepper in rolls. Top with sausages. Stir yogurt until creamy. Spread over sausages. Makes 4 sandwiches.

Rye Pocket Reubens

East meets West in this unbeatable sandwich.

Yellow cornmeal

1 pkg. active dry yeast

1/3 cup warm water (110°F, 45°C)

1 teaspoon salt

1 teaspoon sugar

1/4 teaspoon baking soda

1 tablespoon vegetable oil

1 cup rye flour

2 to 2-1/2 cups all-purpose flour

1 cup plain yogurt

Reuben Fillings, see below

Reuben Fillings:

12 thin slices corned beef

12 (4-inch square) slices Swiss cheese

3/4 cup Thousand Island Dressing, page 51

3/4 cup drained sauerkraut

Butter or margarine for frying

Sprinkle cornmeal on 3 baking sheets. In a large bowl, sprinkle yeast over warm water. Stir to dissolve yeast. Add salt, sugar, baking soda, oil, rye flour, 1 cup of the all-purpose flour and yogurt. Beat until smooth. Stir in enough remaining flour to make dough easy to handle. On a lightly floured surface, knead dough about 8 to 10 minutes until smooth and elastic. Lightly butter bowl. Put dough in bowl and turn to butter top. Cover dough with a damp towel and let rise in a warm place until doubled in bulk, about 1-1/2 hours. Punch down dough. Divide into 6 equal portions. Shape each portion into a ball. Cover and let rise again about 30 minutes. On a lightly floured surface, roll out each ball to a 1/8-inch-thick circle. Place 2 circles in opposite corners of each prepared baking sheet. Cover and let rise about 30 minutes. Prepare Reuben Fillings. Preheat oven to 500°F (260°C). Bake pocket breads 8 to 10 minutes until golden brown and puffy. Cut in half; fill with Reuben Filling. Or place hot bread in plastic bags to keep moist and soft until ready to serve. Makes 6 sandwiches.

Reuben Fillings:

For each half use 1 slice corned beef. Cut cheese slices in half. Place 2 half slices cheese on top of corned beef. Spread each with 1 tablespoon Thousand Island Dressing. Top with sauerkraut. Fold corned beef over. Brush skillet with butter or margarine. Place Reuben fillings in skillet. Cover and heat until warm.

1/Divide risen dough into 6 equal portions and let rise again for 30 minutes before rolling into circles 1/8-inch thick.

How To Make Rye Pocket Reubens

2/After making Reuben Fillings, place in skillet. Cover and heat until warm. Place hot pocket breads in plastic bags to keep moist and soft until ready to serve.

3/Bake pocket breads until browned and puffy. Cut in half and fill with warm filling.

Coney Island Dogs

Use half the sauce for tonight's supper; refrigerate the other half.

1 lb. lean ground beef
1 (1-lb. 13-oz.) can tomato puree
1/4 cup water
1/4 cup sugar
1 teaspoon salt
1/4 teaspoon pepper
Dash garlic salt

1/2 cup plain yogurt, room temperature
1/4 cup sweet relish
2 teaspoons prepared mustard
Buns
Hot Dogs
Water

Brown meat in a large skillet, stirring to break up meat. Drain excess fat. Stir in tomato puree, water, sugar, salt, pepper and garlic salt. Simmer partially covered 45 minutes. Remove from heat. Preheat oven to 350°F (175°C). Stir yogurt until creamy. Gradually blend into sauce. Stir in relish and mustard. Sauce will keep in refrigerator 1 week. Reheat over low heat before serving. Sprinkle buns with water. Wrap in foil and heat in oven 7 minutes. Put hot dogs in a saucepan with 1/2 inch of water. Cover and steam about 5 minutes. Serve with prepared sauce. Makes about 6 cups sauce, enough for 12 to 16 servings.

Super Sloppy Joes

The 30-minute dinner!

1 lb. lean ground beef
1 small onion, minced
1 small green pepper, minced
1 (10-1/2-oz.) can condensed tomato soup
2 teaspoons barbecue sauce
1 teaspoon salt

1 teaspoon brown sugar
1 teaspoon prepared mustard
1/4 teaspoon paprika
1/2 cup plain yogurt, room temperature
6 hamburger buns, cut in half

In a large skillet, brown meat, onion and green pepper about 15 minutes, stirring to break up meat. Stir in tomato soup, barbecue sauce, salt, brown sugar, mustard and paprika. Simmer about 15 minutes until thickened. Remove from heat. In small bowl, stir yogurt until creamy. Stir a small amount of meat mixture into yogurt. Gradually add yogurt-meat mixture to remaining meat mixture. Serve on buns. Makes 6 open-face sandwiches.

Spectacular Heroes

Invite your friends for an after-the-game sandwich.

1 lb. lean ground beef
1 medium onion, chopped
1/4 cup tomato sauce
Few sprigs parsley, chopped
1 teaspoon salt
1/4 teaspoon pepper

1 teaspoon dill weed
2/3 cup plain yogurt, room temperature
1 egg, slightly beaten
1 tablespoon grated Parmesan cheese
4 small French rolls

Preheat oven to 350°F (175°C). In a large skillet, brown meat and onion together about 15 minutes. Drain excess fat. Stir in tomato sauce, parsley, salt, pepper and dill weed. Cook uncovered about 30 minutes until thick. Remove from heat. In a small bowl, stir yogurt until creamy. Blend in egg and Parmesan cheese. Stir into ground beef mixture. Cut a thin slice off top of rolls. Scoop out centers, leaving bread shells. Spoon meat mixture into rolls. Replace tops. Wrap in foil and heat 8 to 10 minutes. Slice before serving. These can be made ahead, refrigerated and warmed in preheated 325°F (165°C) oven 15 minutes before serving. Makes 4 sandwiches.

Terrific Tacos

A must for all taco lovers.

1 lb. lean ground beef
1 (1-1/4-oz.) pkg. taco seasoning mix
3/4 cup water
1 tomato, peeled and diced
1/2 cup (2-oz.) shredded Cheddar cheese

1/4 cup plain yogurt, room temperature
8 taco shells or tostada shells
Shredded lettuce
1/2 cup (2-oz.) shredded Cheddar cheese
1 tomato, peeled and diced

Brown meat in a large skillet, stirring to break up meat. Drain excess fat. Stir in taco seasoning mix and water. Bring to a boil. Reduce heat and simmer uncovered 15 to 20 minutes, stirring occasionally. Add 1 diced tomato and 1/2 cup cheese. Stir until cheese begins to melt. In a small bowl, stir yogurt until creamy. Stir about 1 tablespoon meat mixture into yogurt. Add yogurt-meat mixture to remaining meat. Spoon 3 tablespoons taco filling into bottom of each taco shell or spread on top of each tostada shell. Top with shredded lettuce, 1/2 cup shredded cheese and remaining diced tomato. Makes 8 tacos or tostadas.

Earl of Sandwich

A hearty open-face sandwich resembling the original.

About 2 teaspoons butter or margarine,
  softened
2 large slices pumpernickel bread
Lettuce leaves

8 thin slices cooked roast beef
1 small sweet onion, thinly sliced
1 small tomato, thinly sliced
  Horseradish Sauce, page 114

Spread butter or margarine on bread. Cover with lettuce leaves. Top with roast beef slices. Garnish with onion and tomato slices. Pour Horseradish Sauce over all. Makes 2 open-face sandwiches.

Zucchini Tostadas

Traditionally Mexican—with a flavorful variation.

1 lb. lean ground beef
1 large onion, chopped
1/4 cup chopped celery
1/4 cup diced green pepper
1/8 teaspoon oregano
1/2 cup plain yogurt, room temperature
1/4 cup breadcrumbs
2 medium zucchini, thinly sliced

2 tablespoons vegetable oil
Butter or margarine for frying
About 2 tablespoons butter or margarine,
  softened
6 flour tortillas
1 cup (4-oz.) shredded Cheddar cheese
6 pitted black olives, sliced

Preheat oven to 400°F (205°C). Brown meat slightly in a large skillet, stirring to break up meat. Add onion, celery, green pepper and oregano. Cook until onion is golden. Remove from heat. In a small bowl, stir yogurt until creamy. Add breadcrumbs. Stir a small amount of meat mixture into yogurt. Gradually add yogurt-meat mixture to remaining meat mixture. Put zucchini on large baking sheet. Drizzle with oil. Bake 10 minutes. Turn zucchini slices and bake another 10 minutes until browned. In a small skillet, add enough butter or margarine to cover bottom. Brush 1 side of a tortilla with softened butter or margarine. Fry about 1 to 2 minutes on each side until golden brown. Repeat with remaining tortillas. Put tortillas on a large baking sheet. Place an equal amount of cooked zucchini on each tortilla. Divide meat mixture evenly over zucchini. Top with Cheddar cheese. Bake 15 minutes until golden brown. Top with black olives. Makes 6 tostadas.

Super Gyros

Inspired by the classic Greek sandwich.

2 lbs. lean ground lamb
1/4 cup water
1/4 cup grated onion
2 tablespoons minced parsley
1 teaspoon oregano
1/4 teaspoon garlic powder
3/4 teaspoon pepper

2 teaspoons salt
1 teaspoon ground cumin
1/2 teaspoon ground fenugreek
8 pocket breads
1/2 cup plain yogurt
1 large chopped sweet onion
1 large tomato, thinly sliced

Line a 9" x 5" loaf pan with plastic wrap, overlapping the edges. In a large bowl, mix ground lamb, water, onion, parsley, oregano, garlic powder, pepper, salt, cumin and fenugreek. Shape into a loaf and place in prepared pan. Cover top of loaf with plastic wrap and put 2 or 3 layers of cardboard on top. You need weight to press loaf down. Unopened 16-ounce cans work well. Refrigerate 1 to 2 hours. Preheat oven to 350°F (175°C). Carefully remove loaf from pan and place on a 1-inch-deep baking sheet. Bake 1 to 1-1/4 hours until browned. Remove from oven and drain excess fat. Let stand 10 minutes before slicing. Wrap pocket bread in foil. Place in hot oven to warm. Stir yogurt until creamy. Carve lamb loaf diagonally in very thin slices. Fill pocket bread with sliced lamb loaf, onion and tomato. Top with yogurt. Makes 8 sandwiches.

Variation
Substitute 2 pounds lean ground beef for ground lamb.

Create new sandwich spreads by combining Yogo-Cheese, page 161, with different herbs.

Main Dishes

International favorite sauces and gravies are outstanding with yogurt. When you serve Sauerbraten, Lamb Shanks a la Grecque or Veal Viennese, everyone will want to know what the secret ingredient is! You'll enjoy the delicate taste of yogurt gravy over Savory Roast Chicken. Yogurt is a wonderful tenderizer for the thrifty chuck steaks. Try Leilani Chuck Steak with its yogurt marinade.

Yogurt blends well with easy-on-the-budget main dishes. Stir a little yogurt into the gravy for Old-Style Beef Stew, Salisbury Steak or Oven Pot Roast. The results are superb!

Many recipes in this book require stirring a little of the hot soup, sauce or gravy into the yogurt before adding it to the hot liquid to prevent curdling. But you can stir yogurt directly into the sauce or gravy when a binding agent such as flour or cornstarch is present or the amount of yogurt used is very small. Stir the yogurt very gradually and carefully into the sauce or gravy.

I used Homemade Plain Yogurt, page 13, in all the main dish recipes. You can use homemade Plain Yogurt, Whole Milk Yogurt or store-bought unflavored yogurt. Before adding yogurt to hot gravy, stir the yogurt with a whisk. Creamy yogurt makes a smoother gravy.

CHICKEN JUBILEE
Yogurt-Glazed Chicken, page 79
Fluffy Buttered Rice, page 101
Brussels Sprouts
Citrus Salad
Spice Cake
Coffee or Tea

CANTONESE DINNER
Won Ton Soup
Shrimp Egg Rolls With Mustard Sauce
Stir-Fried Beef & Almond Rice, page 86
Lettuce, Water Chestnut & Crabmeat Salad
With Soy Dressing
Fortune Cookies
Tea

TURKISH DELIGHT
Classic Yogurt Dip, page 38
Shish Kebabs & Rice, page 84
Mixed Green Salad
Honey-Nut Torte
Turkish Coffee

THE STEW KETTLE
Old-Style Beef Stew, page 70
Endive & Beet Salad
Rye Bread
Cheesecake
Tea or Coffee

Monday's Meat Loaf

Start off the week with this delicious low-cost recipe.

Tomato Topping, see below
1-1/2 lbs. lean ground beef
3 slices frozen white bread, crumbled
1/4 cup minced onion
1/2 cup plain yogurt
2 eggs, slightly beaten
3 tablespoons minced parsley

1-1/2 teaspoons salt
1/4 teaspoon pepper
1/4 teaspoon garlic powder
1/4 teaspoon celery salt
2 teaspoons Worcestershire sauce
3 hard-cooked eggs

Tomato Topping:
1 cup plain yogurt, room temperature
1 (10-3/4-oz.) can tomato soup

2 tablespoons ketchup

Prepare Tomato Topping. Preheat oven to 350°F (175°C) Lightly grease an 11" x 7" baking pan. Set aside. Line a 9" x 5" loaf pan with wax paper. In a large bowl, lightly mix meat, breadcrumbs, onion, yogurt, 2 beaten eggs, parsley, salt, pepper, garlic powder, celery salt and Worcestershire sauce. Gently pat 2/3 of the meat mixture into prepared loaf pan. With fingers make an indentation down center of meat. Place 3 whole hard-cooked eggs in indentation. Pat remaining meat over eggs. Unmold into prepared baking pan. Spread 1/3 cup Tomato Topping evenly over loaf. Bake 1 hour. Just before serving, add 2 tablespoons meat loaf drippings to remaining Tomato Topping. Heat to serving temperature. Slice meat loaf. Pour Tomato Topping over individual servings. Makes about 6 servings.

Tomato Topping:
In a small saucepan, stir yogurt until creamy. Blend in tomato soup and ketchup. Mix well.

Freeze leftover stale bread and use it in meat loaf. It's easier to crumble the bread before it's completely thawed.

Old-Style Beef Stew

You'll recognize the recipe but you won't believe the taste!

2 tablespoons vegetable oil
2 lbs. beef stew meat,
   cut in 1-1/2-inch cubes
2 teaspoons salt
1/8 teaspoon pepper
2 cups water
1 (10-1/2-oz.) can beef consommé
6 small onions, peeled

4 medium potatoes, peeled and quartered
4 carrots, peeled and thinly sliced
6 (10-inch) pieces celery,
   cut in 2-inch lengths
2 tablespoons all-purpose flour
2 tablespoons water
1 cup plain yogurt, room temperature

Heat oil in a Dutch oven or large pot. Add meat and brown well on all sides. Add salt, pepper, water and beef consommé. Cover and simmer about 1-1/2 hours until meat is almost tender. Add onions, potatoes, carrots and celery. Cover and cook 30 more minutes until vegetables are tender. With a slotted spoon remove meat and vegetables to a warm serving platter. Mix flour and water. Stir into hot liquid in pot. Cook about 5 minutes, stirring until gravy is thickened. Stir yogurt until creamy. Slowly blend into hot gravy. Pour gravy over stew. Makes 4 to 6 servings.

Beef-Onion Stew

A favorite in Greece.

1/3 cup vegetable oil
2 lbs. lean chuck or rump,
   cut in 1-inch cubes
3 lbs. small onions
1 tablespoon mixed pickling spice
2 garlic cloves, halved
1 small bay leaf
1 (6-oz.) can tomato paste
1-1/4 cups hot water

1/2 cup vinegar
1 tablespoon salt
1/4 teaspoon pepper
1 teaspoon cornstarch
1 tablespoon cold water
1/2 cup plain yogurt, room temperature
About 3 cups mashed potatoes or
   cooked rice

Heat oil in a Dutch oven or heavy pot. Brown meat slowly about 20 minutes. Peel onions. Tie pickling spice, garlic and bay leaf in a 2-inch square of cheesecloth. Place in pot. Put whole onions on top of meat. In a medium bowl, mix tomato paste and hot water; add vinegar, salt and pepper. Pour over meat and onions. Liquid should cover half the contents of the pot. If not, add more hot water. Place a heavy heatproof plate upside-down over meat and onions to keep the onions intact while cooking. Bring to a boil. Cover and simmer 2 hours until meat and onions are tender. Remove plate and spice bag. With a slotted spoon, place meat and onions on a large warm serving platter. Mix cornstarch with cold water. Stir into sauce. Cook about 5 minutes until thickened. Stir yogurt until creamy. Slowly blend yogurt into hot gravy. Pour gravy over meat and onions. Serve with mashed potatoes or rice. Makes about 6 servings.

Steak a la Mancha

Don Quixote would have loved this Spanish-style steak.

3 lbs. round steak,
  cut 1/2-inch thick
Freshly ground pepper
1 garlic clove, pressed
2 teaspoons salt
1/2 cup all-purpose flour
2 tablespoons olive oil
2 large tomatoes, peeled,
  seeded and chopped
1 small green pepper, diced

1 medium onion, chopped
1 (3-inch) piece of celery, chopped
Few sprigs parsley, minced
1/2 teaspoon sugar
1/4 cup dry red wine
2 tablespoons water
1 to 2 tablespoons all-purpose flour
1/2 cup plain yogurt, room temperature
3 to 4 cups cooked rice

Cut meat into serving pieces. Rub with freshly ground pepper and pressed garlic. Sprinkle with salt and dredge in flour. Heat olive oil in a large skillet. Add meat and brown slowly on both sides. Mix tomatoes, green pepper, onion, celery, parsley, sugar and wine. Pour over meat. Cover and simmer 2 hours until meat is tender. With a slotted spoon, remove meat to a warm serving platter. Add water to flour to make a smooth paste. Blend into sauce in skillet. Cook about 5 minutes, stirring constantly, until thickened. Remove from heat. Stir yogurt until creamy. Gradually stir into hot gravy. Pour over steak and serve with rice. Makes 6 to 8 servings.

Leilani Chuck Steak

Pour the marinade over the steak in the morning and come home to a fast gourmet meal.

1 cup plain yogurt
3 tablespoons soy sauce
1 garlic clove, pressed

1/4 cup vegetable oil
2 lbs. chuck steak, 1-inch thick

In a small bowl, beat yogurt, soy sauce and garlic. Drizzle oil into mixture, stirring constantly. Pierce both sides of steak with a fork. Place in a shallow dish. Pour marinade over steak. Cover and refrigerate 8 to 10 hours. Drain marinade and set aside. Grill or broil steak to desired doneness, brushing frequently with marinade. Makes 4 to 6 servings.

Variation

Marinate tender steaks like sirloin, T-bone, porterhouse or rib eye only 2 to 3 hours before grilling or broiling.

Salisbury Steak

Easy and economical.

1-1/2 lbs. lean ground beef
1/2 cup fine dry breadcrumbs
2 eggs, slightly beaten
1 (10-1/2-oz.) can condensed onion soup
2 tablespoons ketchup
1/4 teaspoon salt
1/8 teaspoon pepper
2 tablespoons vegetable oil

1 tablespoon flour
1/4 cup ketchup
1/2 cup beef broth
1 teaspoon Worcestershire sauce
1/4 teaspoon dry mustard
1 teaspoon sugar
1/2 cup plain yogurt, room temperature
About 3 cups mashed potatoes

In a large bowl, lightly mix meat, breadcrumbs, eggs, 1/3 cup of the soup, 2 tablespoons ketchup, salt and pepper. Shape into 6 oval patties. Heat oil in a large skillet. Brown patties. Drain excess fat. In a small bowl, gradually blend remaining soup into flour. Stir in 1/4 cup ketchup, beef broth, Worcestershire sauce, mustard and sugar. Pour into skillet. Stir to loosen browned bits. Cover and cook over low heat 40 minutes. In a small bowl, stir yogurt until creamy. Blend a small amount of hot sauce into yogurt. Gradually stir yogurt mixture into sauce. Keep warm on low heat. Serve with mashed potatoes. Makes about 6 servings.

Ground Chuck Steaks

Golden yogurt sauce enhances hamburgers.

1/4 cup butter or margarine
1 large onion, thinly sliced
1/2 green pepper, sliced lengthwise
2 tablespoons all-purpose flour

1 (10-1/2-oz.) can beef consommé
1 cup plain yogurt, room temperature
6 lean ground chuck patties

Melt butter or margarine in a small saucepan. Add onion, green pepper and flour. Sauté until onion is golden brown, stirring often. Stir in beef consommé. Cook about 5 minutes until thickened. Stir yogurt until creamy. Stir into sauce. Heat to serving temperature. Broil or fry beef patties. Spoon warm sauce over patties. Makes about 6 servings.

Variation

Serve the sauce over steaks or meat loaf.

Sauerbraten

A bit of nostalgia in every bite.

4 lbs. beef sirloin tip roast	1 teaspoon flour
Beef Marinade, see below	1 tablespoon brown sugar
2 teaspoons salt	3/4 cup water
1/4 teaspoon pepper	2/3 cup crumbled ginger snaps
2 tablespoons vegetable oil	1/2 cup plain yogurt, room temperature

Beef Marinade:

1 large onion	7 whole cloves
1/2 cup plain yogurt, room temperature	7 peppercorns
2-1/2 cups water	2 small bay leaves
1/2 cup vinegar	1/3 cup vegetable oil
1 tablespoon brown sugar	

Put meat in large bowl. Prepare Beef Marinade and pour over meat. Cover and refrigerate 8 to 10 hours, turning at least once. Remove meat from marinade and pat dry. Sprinkle with salt and pepper. Strain marinade and set aside. Heat oil in a Dutch oven or heavy pot. Brown meat slowly on all sides and pour off excess drippings. In a small bowl, blend 1 teaspoon flour with 2 tablespoons of marinade. Stir into marinade and pour over meat. Cover and cook 2 hours until meat is tender. Place meat on a warm platter. Pour off gravy. Measure 2 cups and pour back into pot. Stir in brown sugar and water. Bring to a boil. Add crumbled gingersnaps. Cook about 5 minutes, stirring until thickened. In a small bowl, stir yogurt until creamy. Very carefully blend a small amount of hot gravy into yogurt. Gradually add yogurt-gravy mixture to remaining gravy. Serve gravy with roast. Makes about 8 servings.

Beef Marinade:

Thinly slice onion into a medium heatproof bowl; set aside. In a 1-quart saucepan, stir yogurt until creamy. Blend in water, vinegar, brown sugar, cloves, peppercorns and bay leaves. Bring to a boil. Pour over sliced onion and cool. Gradually drizzle in oil, stirring constantly.

Variation

Substitute rolled rump roast, beef blade steak, beef chuck pot roast or beef brisket for sirloin tip roast.

Oven Pot Roast & Yogurt Gravy

Don't tell them the secret of your extra-special gravy.

1 (3-1/2-lb.) beef pot roast
1 teaspoon salt
1/8 teaspoon pepper
2 garlic cloves, minced
1 (10-1/2-oz.) can beef consommé
1/2 cup minced onion

1 bay leaf
1 tablespoon brown sugar
1 teaspoon water
1/2 teaspoon cornstarch
1/2 cup plain yogurt, room temperature
Salt and pepper to taste

Preheat oven to 325°F (165°C). Sprinkle meat with salt and pepper. Put meat on a small rack in a Dutch oven or large pot. Sprinkle meat with minced garlic. Add consommé, onion, bay leaf and brown sugar. Cover and roast 3-1/2 to 4 hours until meat is tender. Remove meat to a warm serving platter. Slice and keep warm. Discard bay leaf. Place pot over low heat. Mix water and cornstarch. Blend into hot sauce in pot. Stir until thickened. Remove from heat. Stir yogurt until creamy. Gradually blend into hot gravy. Season with more salt and pepper to taste. Pour gravy immediately over sliced pot roast. Makes about 6 servings.

Veal Viennese

After dinner make a potful of spicy Viennese coffee.

4 thin veal cutlets (about 1 lb.)
1/2 teaspoon salt
1/8 teaspoon white pepper
3 tablespoons butter or margarine
1 tablespoon vegetable oil
1 green onion, thinly sliced
1 teaspoon minced parsley
1/2 teaspoon oregano

1/2 teaspoon basil
1/3 cup dry white wine
1 tablespoon all-purpose flour
2 tablespoons water
1/2 cup plain yogurt, room temperature
Bavarian Spaetzle, page 101, or
    2 cups cooked noodles

Sprinkle cutlets with salt and white pepper. Heat butter or margarine and oil in a large skillet. Brown cutlets on both sides. Add green onion, parsley, oregano, basil and wine. Cover and simmer 10 minutes. With slotted spoon, place cutlets on a warm serving platter; keep warm. Blend flour and water. Stir into sauce. Cook about 5 minutes, stirring constantly until thickened. Stir yogurt until creamy. With gravy on low heat, gradually add yogurt. Heat gravy to serving temperature. Pour over veal. Serve with Bavarian Spaetzle or cooked noodles. Makes about 4 servings.

Stuffed Chicken Thighs

Ham-stuffed chicken, sealed in golden pastry and served in creamy mushroom sauce.

2 tablespoons butter or margarine	1/4 teaspoon salt
6 chicken thighs, skinned	Dash white pepper
1 chicken bouillon cube	1 (10-oz.) can condensed
1/2 cup boiling water	cream of mushroom soup
2 slices boiled ham,	1 (4-oz.) can sliced mushrooms, drained
cut in julienne strips	1 (10-oz.) pkg. frozen patty shells,
1 tablespoon cornstarch	thawed (6 shells)
1/2 teaspoon paprika	1/2 cup plain yogurt, room temperature

Preheat oven to 400°F (205°C). Melt butter or margarine in a large skillet. Brown chicken evenly on all sides. Dissolve bouillon cube in boiling water. Pour over chicken. Cover and simmer about 30 minutes until chicken is tender. Remove chicken from broth; cool. Carefully remove and discard bones. Put ham strips in the bone cavity of each thigh. Measure broth in pan and add enough water to make 1 cup liquid. Pour back into skillet. In a small bowl, mix cornstarch, paprika, salt and pepper. Add cream of mushroom soup. Add soup mixture to broth. Cook about 5 minutes, stirring until thickened. Stir in mushrooms. On a lightly floured surface, roll out each patty shell to a 6-inch square. Place chicken with ham side up in center of each square. Top with 2 tablespoons sauce. Fold pastry sides over to center and seal edges. Fold ends to center and seal. Place seam-side down in 13" x 9" baking pan. Bake about 30 minutes until golden brown. Heat remaining sauce in skillet. In a small bowl, stir yogurt until creamy. Blend a small amount of hot sauce into yogurt. Gradually add yogurt-sauce mixture to remaining sauce. Heat over low heat. Pour over pastries just before serving. Makes about 6 servings.

Stuffed Cabbage Rolls take on a new look and taste when plain yogurt is spooned over them.

1/Slightly cool chicken thighs before removing bone. Use a paring knife to help separate meat from bone.

How To Make Stuffed Chicken Thighs

2/Place ham strips in bone cavity of each thigh. Prepare patty shells for rolling.

3/Place chicken thighs in center of rolled patty shell squares. Top with about 2 tablespoons sauce. Fold pastry corners to center and seal edges. Place seam-side down in baking pan.

Chicken Curry

Yogurt is right at home with spicy Indian curry.

1 cup uncooked long-grain white rice
1 (2-1/2-lb.) broiler-fryer chicken,
   cut in pieces
3 tablespoons butter or margarine
1 teaspoon curry powder
1 teaspoon paprika

1/4 cup slivered almonds
1/4 cup raisins
1 (10-1/2-oz.) can chicken broth
3/4 cup water
Curry Sauce, see below

Curry Sauce:
1 cup plain yogurt, room temperature
1 (10-3/4-oz.) can cream of chicken soup

1/2 teaspoon curry powder

Preheat oven to 375°F (190°C). Butter a 13" x 9" baking pan. Sprinkle rice evenly on bottom of prepared pan. Top with chicken pieces. Dot with butter or margarine. Sprinkle with curry powder, paprika, almonds and raisins. Pour broth and water over all. Cover and bake 1 hour until chicken is tender. Prepare Curry Sauce. Remove chicken from oven. Arrange on a large serving platter. Pour Curry Sauce over and serve. Makes about 4 servings.

Curry Sauce:
In a small saucepan, stir yogurt until creamy. Blend in cream of chicken soup and curry powder. Heat over low heat to serving temperature.

Peanut Chutney

An exotic yogurt relish to enjoy with curry.

1/2 cup plain yogurt
2 tablespoons water
1 green chili pepper,
   seeded and diced

1/2 cup salted peanuts
1/2 cup flaked coconut
Salt, if desired

Put yogurt, water, chili pepper and half the peanuts in a blender. Cover and blend on high speed about 3 minutes until peanuts are crushed and mixture is smooth. Add remaining peanuts and all of coconut. Continue to blend on high speed until mixture is creamy and smooth. Season with salt, if desired. Makes about 1 cup.

Chicken Paprikash

A taste of tomato sauce and yogurt over chicken.

1-1/2 teaspoons salt
1/2 teaspoon white pepper
1 tablespoon paprika
2 broiler-fryers,
  cut in pieces
2 tablespoons butter or margarine
1 large onion, chopped

1 cup chicken broth
1/4 cup tomato sauce
3 tablespoons all-purpose flour
1/4 cup water
1 cup plain yogurt, room temperature
3 cups hot cooked noodles

Sprinkle salt, pepper and paprika over chicken pieces. Melt butter or margarine in a Dutch oven or large pot. Brown chicken slowly on all sides. Add onion during last few minutes of browning. Stir in chicken broth and tomato sauce. Cover and bring to a boil over high heat. Reduce heat and simmer 1 hour until chicken is tender. Place chicken on a warm serving platter. Mix flour and water. Gradually stir into sauce. Cook about 5 minutes until thickened. In a small bowl, stir yogurt until creamy. Blend a small amount of hot gravy into yogurt. Gradually add yogurt-gravy mixture to remaining sauce. Pour over chicken. Serve with noodles. Makes about 6 servings.

Yogurt-Glazed Chicken

Broiled chicken with a unique glaze.

1/4 teaspoon garlic salt
1/2 teaspoon paprika
1/2 teaspoon basil
1 (2-1/2-lb.) broiler-fryer,
  cut in pieces

1/2 cup plain yogurt, room temperature
1 tablespoon soy sauce
1/2 cup plain yogurt, room temperature
1 teaspoon all-purpose flour
3 tablespoons grated Parmesan cheese

Preheat oven to 400°F (205°C). Sprinkle garlic salt, paprika and basil over chicken pieces. In a small bowl, stir 1/2 cup yogurt and soy sauce until creamy. Place chicken in a shallow baking dish. Brush with yogurt mixture. Bake uncovered 20 minutes. Turn chicken over and baste with juices. Bake another 20 minutes. Reduce oven temperature to 350°F (175°C). In a small bowl, stir 1/2 cup yogurt and flour until creamy. Spread over chicken. Sprinkle cheese over chicken. Bake 3 to 5 minutes. Makes about 4 servings.

Savory Roast Chicken

Delicious with its own creamy gravy.

1 tablespoon vegetable oil	1 (3- to 4-lb.) roasting chicken
1 tablespoon lemon juice	1 (2-inch) piece celery
1 teaspoon salt	1 small lemon wedge
1/8 teaspoon pepper	1/4 cup water
1/2 teaspoon oregano	Creamy Yogurt Gravy, see below

Creamy Yogurt Gravy:

2 tablespoons pan drippings	1 chicken bouillon cube
1 tablespoon all-purpose flour	1 cup plain yogurt, room temperature
1/3 cup water	

Preheat oven to 375°F (190°C). In a small bowl, beat oil, lemon juice, salt, pepper and oregano. Brush entire chicken including cavity with lemon marinade. Place celery and lemon wedge in cavity. Place chicken on rack in a shallow baking pan. Pour water into pan. Roast 2 to 2-1/2 hours until internal temperature reaches 185°F (85°C). Baste chicken occasionally with pan drippings. Prepare Creamy Yogurt Gravy. Remove chicken from oven and place on warm serving platter. Pour gravy over chicken. Makes 4 to 5 servings.

Creamy Yogurt Gravy:
Put 2 tablespoons drippings in a small saucepan. Stir in flour. Cook, stirring until golden. Add water and bouillon cube. Cook about 5 minutes, stirring until thickened. Stir yogurt until creamy. Slowly blend into gravy. Heat to serving temperature.

Pheasant in Cream

Who would think this regal dish could be so easy?

1 (2-1/2- to 3-lb.) pheasant, quartered, or 4 Cornish game hens	1 (10-3/4-oz.) can condensed golden mushroom soup
1 teaspoon salt	1 (4-oz.) can sliced mushrooms, drained
1/8 teaspoon pepper	1/4 cup grated Parmesan cheese
1 cup plain yogurt, room temperature	1/4 cup chopped onion

Preheat oven to 350°F (175°C). Sprinkle pheasant or hens with salt and pepper. Place skin-side up in a single layer in a 13" x 9" baking pan. In a medium bowl, stir yogurt until creamy. Blend in soup, mushrooms, cheese and onion. Spread over pheasant or hens. Bake 1-1/2 to 2 hours until tender, basting occasionally with sauce. Makes about 4 servings.

Diamond Head Spareribs

When you feel like going to Hawaii, cook this.

4 to 6 lbs. country-style spareribs
1 (6-oz.) can thawed frozen
   pineapple juice concentrate

1 small onion, minced
2 tablespoons soy sauce
1/2 cup plain yogurt

Preheat oven to 350°F (175°C). Place spareribs in a shallow baking pan. Cover with aluminum foil. Bake 50 minutes. Remove foil and drain excess fat. Bake 20 more minutes until tender. In a small bowl, beat thawed pineapple juice concentrate, onion, soy sauce and yogurt. Brush ribs with half the pineapple mixture. Bake 7 minutes. Turn ribs and brush with remaining pineapple mixture. Bake 7 more minutes. Makes about 6 servings.

Venison Steaks & Yogurt Gravy

If you're lucky enough to have venison, this recipe is a must!

2 (1-lb.) venison steaks
1 cup plain yogurt, room temperature
1 cup red wine
8 peppercorns
2 bay leaves
6 tablespoons butter or margarine

1 large onion, cut lengthwise in slices
1/2 cup water
1 tablespoon all-purpose flour
1/2 teaspoon salt
1 cup plain yogurt, room temperature

Trim fat from steaks. In a shallow baking dish, stir 1 cup yogurt until creamy. Blend in wine. Add peppercorns and bay leaves. Place venison in marinade. Cover and refrigerate 8 to 10 hours, turning occasionally. Melt butter or margarine in a large skillet. Brown venison on both sides. Add onion during last few minutes of browning. Add water. Cover and cook 1 hour until meat is tender. With a slotted spoon, place venison and onion on a warm platter. Stir flour and salt into drippings. Cook and stir until thick. Stir 1 cup yogurt until creamy. Carefully stir yogurt into gravy. Heat to serving temperature. Makes about 4 servings.

Moussaka

It's worth the extra effort!

1 tablespoon grated Parmesan cheese
2 large eggplants
2 teaspoons salt
Flour for dredging
1/3 cup vegetable oil
1 lb. lean ground beef or ground lamb
2 medium onions, chopped
1 (8-oz.) can tomato sauce
1/2 cup water

1/2 cup minced parsley
1 garlic clove, pressed
1 teaspoon salt
1/4 teaspoon pepper
1/8 teaspoon allspice
3 tablespoons grated Parmesan cheese
1/4 cup plain yogurt, room temperature
Yogurt White Sauce, see below
1 tablespoon grated Parmesan cheese

Yogurt White Sauce:
4 tablespoons butter or margarine
1-1/2 cups cold milk
2 tablespoons cornstarch

Dash salt
2 eggs
1/2 cup plain yogurt, room temperature

Coat a large baking sheet with oil; set aside. Generously butter an 11" x 7" baking pan and sprinkle with 1 tablespoon cheese. Set aside. Peel eggplants, leaving on some strips of skin. Cut lengthwise into 1/4-inch thick slices. Sprinkle with 2 teaspoons salt. Strain in a colander 20 minutes. Rinse off salt and lightly squeeze slices to remove excess water. Dredge in flour and place on prepared baking sheet. Drizzle oil over top. Broil about 10 minutes on each side until golden brown. In a large skillet, brown meat and onions, stirring to break up meat. Add tomato sauce, water, parsley, garlic, 1 teaspoon salt, pepper and allspice. Simmer about 20 minutes. Remove from heat. Stir in 3 table-spoons cheese. In a medium bowl, stir yogurt until creamy. Gradually add to hot meat mixture. Place half the eggplant slices on cheese in buttered baking pan. Spread meat mixture on top. Cover with remaining eggplant. Prepare Yogurt White Sauce. Pour over meat mixture. Sprinkle with 1 tablespoon cheese. Preheat oven to 350°F (175°C). Bake 30 to 40 minutes until golden brown. Cool 10 minutes before serving. Makes about 6 servings.

Yogurt White Sauce:
In a medium saucepan over low heat, cook butter or margarine, milk and cornstarch about 15 minutes, stirring until thickened. Add salt. Remove from heat and cool slightly. Beat eggs in a small bowl. Stir yogurt until creamy. Beat into eggs. Stir a small amount of hot sauce into egg mixture. Gradually add egg mixture to sauce.

Pastitsio

A favorite in my family for many years.

1 tablespoon grated Parmesan cheese
3 quarts water
1 tablespoon salt
3/4 lb. 10-inch long, thick macaroni,
  broken in half, or jumbo elbow macaroni
1-1/2 lbs. lean ground beef or
  ground lamb
2 medium onions, chopped
3 tablespoons tomato paste
1/4 cup water

1 teaspoon salt
1/4 teaspoon pepper
1/4 teaspoon cinnamon
1/8 teaspoon nutmeg
1/4 cup plain yogurt, room temperature
4 tablespoons butter or margerine, melted
3/4 cup grated Parmesan cheese
1 egg, beaten
Yogurt Cream Sauce, see below
2 tablespoons grated Parmesan cheese

Yogurt Cream Sauce:
4 tablespoons butter or margarine
2-1/2 cups cold milk
4 tablespoons cornstarch

Dash salt
4 eggs
1 cup plain yogurt, room temperature

Preheat oven to 350°F (175°C). Generously butter a 13" x 9" baking pan. Sprinkle 1 tablespoon cheese over bottom of pan. In a large pot, bring 3 quarts water and 1 tablespoon salt to a boil. Add macaroni. Boil 10 minutes. Drain macaroni and rinse with cold water; set aside. Brown meat and onions in a large skillet, stirring to break up meat. Add tomato paste, 1/4 cup water, 1 teaspoon salt, pepper, cinnamon and nutmeg. Simmer about 10 minutes. Remove from heat. Stir yogurt until creamy. Gradually add to hot meat mixture. Pour melted butter or margarine over cooked macaroni. Toss 3/4 cup grated Parmesan cheese and beaten egg with macaroni. Spread half the macaroni mixture in prepared pan. Cover with meat mixture. Top with remaining macaroni. Prepare Yogurt Cream Sauce. Pour over macaroni. Sprinkle with 2 tablespoons grated Parmesan cheese. Bake 45 minutes until golden brown. Makes about 6 servings.

Yogurt Cream Sauce:
In a medium saucepan over low heat, cook butter or margarine, milk and cornstarch about 15 minutes, stirring until thickened. Add salt. Remove from heat and cool slightly. Beat eggs in a small bowl. Stir yogurt until creamy. Beat into eggs. Stir a small amount of hot sauce into egg mixture. Gradually add egg mixture to sauce.

Shish Kebabs & Rice

An exotic dish to make and serve on your patio.

Fluffy Buttered Rice, page 101
2 lbs. lean lamb,
　cut in 1-1/2-inch cubes
1 cup plain yogurt
Juice of 1 lemon
2 teaspoons oregano
1/8 teaspoon freshly ground pepper
1 garlic clove, pressed

1/4 cup olive oil
2 large green peppers
1 onion, quartered
2 teaspoons salt
12 mushroom caps
12 cherry tomatoes
Brandy for flaming, if desired

Prepare Fluffy Buttered Rice. While rice is cooking, place lamb cubes in a shallow baking dish. In a small bowl, beat yogurt, lemon juice, oregano, pepper and garlic. Gradually drizzle olive oil into yogurt mixture and beat well. Pour over lamb cubes. Cover and refrigerate about 4 hours. Cut green peppers lengthwise into thirds and remove seeds. Cut again into thirds crosswise. Peel onion quarters into 2 layer sections. Remove lamb cubes from marinade. Sprinkle with salt. Alternate lamb, green pepper, mushroom caps, tomatoes and onions on skewers. Brush with marinade. Broil about 15 minutes over medium heat. Turn heat on high and cook 7 to 10 more minutes. If desired, warm brandy over medium heat. Ignite. Pour flaming brandy over kebabs. Serve with Fluffy Buttered Rice. Makes 4 to 6 servings.

Lamb Shanks a la Grecque

A tangy egg-yogurt sauce finishes off this Mediterranean dish.

4 lamb shanks, cut in half
2 teaspoons salt
1/2 teaspoon white pepper
2 tablespoons vegetable oil
1 medium onion, chopped
1 cup water

1 medium bunch celery,
　cut in 2-inch pieces
3 egg yolks
1 tablespoon cornstarch
1/2 cup plain yogurt, room temperature

Sprinkle lamb shanks with salt and white pepper. Heat oil in a Dutch oven or large pot. Brown lamb shanks evenly on all sides in hot oil. Stir in onion during last few minutes of browning. Pour in water. Cover and cook 1 hour. Add celery. Cook 45 more minutes until celery is tender. In a medium bowl, beat egg yolks and cornstarch with an electric mixer on high speed until thick. Stir yogurt until creamy. Gradually blend into beaten yolks. Blend a small amount of hot broth from the lamb into the egg mixture. Gradually stir egg mixture into broth, blending well. Cover pot and shake gently to distribute sauce. Serve immediately. To reheat, heat to serving temperature over very low heat. Do not boil or sauce may curdle. Makes about 4 servings.

Stir-Fried Lamb & Almond Rice

Here's a fast-cooking dish to prepare in your wok.

Almond Rice, see below
2 bunches green onions
1 lb. lean boneless leg of lamb,
   partially frozen (about 2 cups sliced)
3 tablespoons soy sauce
2 tablespoons sherry
1/2 teaspoon sugar

1 teaspoon cornstarch
1/4 cup vegetable oil
2 small garlic cloves, minced
1 tablespoon soy sauce
1 teaspoon vinegar
1 cup plain yogurt, room temperature

Almond Rice:
3 tablespoons butter or margarine
1/2 cup slivered almonds
1 cup uncooked long grain rice

2-1/2 cups chicken broth
1/2 teaspoon salt
1/4 teaspoon sugar

Prepare Almond Rice. While rice is cooking, trim each green onion. Discard ends and outer layers. Wash and drain. Cut in 2-inch lengths and shred finely. Thinly slice lamb. Cut in 1/2" x 2" strips. In a medium bowl, combine sliced lamb, 3 tablespoons soy sauce, sherry, sugar and cornstarch. Mix well. Heat wok on high heat 30 seconds. Add oil and rotate wok to coat with oil. Add garlic and lamb. Stir and cook until lamb browns slightly. Add shredded green onions, 1 tablespoon soy sauce and vinegar. Toss and stir with lamb 2 to 3 minutes. Place lamb in center of a warm platter. Surround with Almond Rice. Stir yogurt until creamy. Spoon over rice. Serve immediately. Makes about 4 servings.

Almond Rice:

Melt butter or margarine in a 2-quart saucepan. Add almonds and sauté until lightly browned. Add rice. Sauté 2 to 3 minutes. Stir in chicken broth, salt and sugar. Cover and simmer 20 minutes. Remove from heat. Let stand covered about 5 minutes until all liquid is absorbed.

Variation

Substitute Beef Tenderloin for lamb.

Stir plain yogurt until creamy and spread over broiled hamburgers for flavor variety.

Casseroles & Vegetables

Recipes for blending yogurt with tuna, ham, poultry, frankfurters or other foods in delicious casseroles could fill another cookbook!

Most casseroles are a complete meal. With a salad, bread and dessert they become a hearty dinner. Casseroles are economical, too. Leftover chicken, turkey, beef or ham with pasta or rice are quick to prepare, nutritious and flavorful. When I shop for meat or poultry, I buy the largest piece available. This way I have some left over for a casserole. Use leftover chicken in Crunchy Chicken Casserole, or ham in Ham au Gratin. They are delicious and save you money too.

Yogurt should be at room temperature when it's added to casseroles. In dishes like Texas Hash or Quick Chili, add a little of the hot food to the yogurt first and then gradually blend the mixture into the main dish.

For a casserole topping I developed Quick Yogurt Glaze which can be spooned over any casserole during the last 20 minutes of baking. Try it first over Ratatouille.

Discover how compatible yogurt is with canned condensed soups in Turkey Divan or Nifty Noodle Bake. For a spirited new taste, spoon yogurt over baked potatoes, toss with pasta or use as a topping for rice. You'll enjoy this low-calorie gourmet touch!

FOR VEGETABLE LOVERS
Ratatouille, page 94
Quick Yogurt Glaze, page 103
Cheese Wedges
Celery Fans
Carrot Curls
Plain Yogurt
Coffee

COMPANY FOR DINNER
Roast Leg of Lamb
Mint Pears
Continental Stuffed Vegetables, page 96
Endive Salad
Hot Dinner Rolls
Banana Pie
Tea

BUSY DAY BAKE
Cheese & Tuna Casserole, page 93
Leafy Green Salad
Hot Rolls
Spiced Peaches
Lemonade

AUTUMN DINNER
Turkey Divan, page 92
Assorted Relishes
Cranberry Nut Mold
Crescent Rolls
Pumpkin Spice Cake
Tea

Ham au Gratin

It has a mellow old-fashioned flavor.

1/4 cup vegetable oil
1 (1-lb.) pkg. frozen hash brown
  potatoes with onions
1 (1-lb.) ham steak,
  cut in julienne strips

1 cup plain yogurt, room temperature
1 (11-oz.) can Cheddar cheese soup
1/2 teaspoon prepared mustard
1/2 teaspoon salt
1/8 teaspoon white pepper

Preheat oven to 350°F (175°C). Butter a 9-inch square baking pan. Set aside. Heat oil in a large skillet. Add hash browns. Cover and cook 4 minutes. Uncover and cook 8 more minutes until golden brown. Put in prepared baking pan. Place ham strips over potatoes. Reserve about 1/4 cup ham strips for topping. In a medium bowl, stir yogurt until creamy. Blend in soup, mustard, salt and white pepper. Pour over casserole. Arrange reserved ham strips over top. Bake 20 to 25 minutes until golden brown. Makes about 4 servings.

Frankaroni

Frankfurter slices in a velvety cheese sauce.

1 (7-oz.) pkg. macaroni
Water
1 lb. frankfurters
2/3 cup plain yogurt, room temperature

1 (11-oz.) can condensed Cheddar cheese soup
1 teaspoon dry mustard
1/2 cup thinly sliced green onions
1/2 cup crushed cracker crumbs

Preheat oven to 350°F (175°C). Generously butter a shallow 2-quart casserole. Set aside. Cook macaroni in water according to package directions. Drain. Slice frankfurters diagonally into bite-size pieces. In a small bowl, stir yogurt until creamy. Blend in soup and dry mustard. In a large bowl, mix macaroni, frankfurters, yogurt-soup mixture and onions. Put in prepared casserole. Sprinkle crushed cracker crumbs over top. Bake about 30 minutes until golden brown. Makes about 5 servings.

To make herb-seasoned croutons, cube 3 slices white bread. Melt 2 tablespoons butter in a small skillet. Add bread cubes. Sprinkle with 1/8 teaspoon each thyme, basil, oregano and Italian herbs. Sauté until croutons are golden.

Ham au Gratin

Quick Chili

A great thick chili.

1 tablespoon vegetable oil	1 to 2 teaspoons chili powder
1 lb. lean ground beef	1/2 teaspoon cumin
1 onion, minced	Dash garlic powder
3/4 cup water	Tabasco® sauce to taste
1 (16-oz.) can pinto beans	1/2 cup plain yogurt, room temperature
1 tablespoon ketchup	

Heat oil in a large skillet. Add meat and onion. Cook until meat is browned, stirring to break up meat. Add water, pinto beans, ketchup, chili powder, cumin and garlic powder. Stir in a few drops Tabasco® sauce to taste. Bring to a boil. Reduce heat and simmer uncovered 10 minutes. In a small bowl, stir yogurt until creamy. Blend a small amount of hot chili into yogurt. Gradually add yogurt-chili mixture to remaining chili. Serve immediately. Chili will curdle if reheated but this will not affect the flavor. Makes about 4 servings.

Fiesta Dinner

Ready in a jiffy. You'll even have time to whip up some corn bread.

2 tablespoons vegetable oil	1 teaspoon salt
1 lb. lean ground beef	1/8 teaspoon pepper
1 small onion, chopped	Dash garlic powder
1/2 cup chopped celery	1-1/3 cups cooked long-grain rice
1/2 green pepper, minced	1 (4-oz.) can peas, drained
1 (8-oz.) can tomato sauce	1/2 cup plain yogurt, room temperature
1-1/2 cups beef broth	1 teaspoon cornstarch
1 teaspoon sugar	Minced parsley

Heat oil in a large skillet. Add beef, onion, celery and green pepper. Cook over high heat about 5 minutes until meat is browned, stirring to break up meat. Add tomato sauce, broth, sugar, salt, pepper and garlic powder. Cover and simmer 8 minutes. Stir in cooked rice and peas. Cover and heat 3 to 5 minutes. Remove from heat. In a small bowl, blend yogurt and cornstarch until smooth and creamy. Gradually add yogurt mixture to meat mixture. Sprinkle with parsley. Serve immediately. Makes 4 to 6 servings.

Texas Hash

A robust meal for hearty appetites.

1-1/2 lbs. lean ground beef
1 small onion, chopped
1-1/2 cups cooked long-grain rice
1 (16-oz.) can lima beans, drained
1 (8-oz.) can green beans, drained
1 (8-oz.) can corn, drained

1 (10-1/2-oz.) can tomato bisque soup
1/2 cup beef broth
1 teaspoon chili powder
1 teaspoon black pepper
1 cup plain yogurt, room temperature

In a Dutch oven or large pot, brown meat and onion, stirring to break up meat. Add rice, lima beans, green beans, corn, soup, broth, chili powder and pepper. Mix well. Cover and simmer 20 minutes. Remove from heat. In a small bowl, stir yogurt until creamy. Blend a small amount of hash into yogurt. Gradually add yogurt-hash mixture to remaining hash. Serve immediately. Hash will curdle if reheated but this will not affect the flavor. Makes 6 to 8 servings.

Nifty Noodle Bake

A tasty, economical casserole.

8 oz. uncooked noodles
Water
1-1/2 lbs. lean ground beef
1 medium onion, chopped
2 teaspoons salt
1/2 teaspoon pepper
1 cup plain yogurt, room temperature

1 (10-1/2-oz.) can condensed
   cream of mushroom soup
1 (16-oz.) can green beans, drained
1 (4-oz.) can mushroom stems and pieces,
   drained
2 tablespoons minced pimiento, drained
1 cup shredded Cheddar cheese

Preheat oven to 350°F (175°C). Generously butter a 3-quart casserole. Set aside. Cook noodles in water according to package directions. Drain and set aside. In a large skillet, brown beef, onion, salt and pepper, stirring to break up meat. In a large bowl, stir yogurt until creamy. Blend in soup. Add browned beef, cooked noodles, green beans, mushrooms, pimiento and 1/2 cup cheese. Mix well. Pour into prepared casserole. Sprinkle with remaining cheese. Bake 20 to 30 minutes until cheese is golden brown. Makes about 6 servings.

Crunchy Chicken Casserole

A beautiful blend of crisp textures.

1 cup plain yogurt, room temperature
1 (10-oz.) can cream of celery soup
1 teaspoon soy sauce
3 tablespoons butter or margarine
2 cups diced chicken

1/2 cup diced celery
1/2 cup sliced water chestnuts
1 tablespoon minced onion
1 (3-oz.) can chow mein noodles
1/4 cup toasted slivered almonds

Preheat oven to 350°F (175°C). Generously butter a 2-quart casserole. Set aside. In a small bowl, stir yogurt until creamy. Blend in soup and soy sauce. Melt butter or margarine in a large skillet. Add chicken, celery, water chestnuts and onion. Sauté about 5 minutes until golden. Remove from heat. Add chow mein noodles and toss. Put in prepared casserole. Pour yogurt mixture over all. Sprinkle with almonds. Bake about 30 minutes until golden brown. Makes about 4 servings.

Turkey Divan

Try this with leftover turkey or chicken.

2 (10-oz.) pkgs. frozen broccoli spears
Water
1 cup plain yogurt, room temperature
2 (10-1/2-oz.) cans cream of chicken soup

4 cups cubed cooked turkey
3/4 cup shredded Cheddar cheese (3-oz.)
1/2 cup cheese cracker crumbs

Preheat oven to 350°F (175°C). Butter a 13" x 9" baking pan. Set aside. Cook broccoli in water according to package directions. Drain. In a medium saucepan, stir yogurt until creamy. Blend in soup. Place broccoli in prepared baking pan. Top with turkey. Pour yogurt mixture over turkey and sprinkle with Cheddar cheese. Top with cracker crumbs. Bake 30 minutes until golden brown. Makes about 8 servings.

Variation
Substitute cubed cooked chicken for the turkey.

Cheese & Tuna Casserole

Had a busy day? Try this energy-packed casserole.

1 cup plain yogurt, room temperature
2 tablespoons vegetable oil
1 (10-oz.) can cream of celery soup
2 (6-1/2-oz.) cans tuna fish,
   drained and flaked
2 cups cooked long-grain rice

1 (8-oz.) can peas, drained
1 cup chopped celery
12 black olives, sliced
1 tablespoon minced parsley
1 tablespoon minced onion
4 slices processed American cheese

Preheat oven to 350°F (175°C). Butter a 2-quart casserole. In a large bowl, stir yogurt until creamy. Drizzle oil into yogurt stirring constantly. Add soup, tuna fish, rice, peas, celery, olives, parsley and onion. Put in prepared casserole. Bake about 25 minutes. Remove from oven and arrange cheese slices over top. Bake 5 more minutes until cheese melts. Makes about 6 servings.

Variation

Substitute 1-1/2 cups cubed cooked chicken for tuna fish.

Tuna Bake

The babysitter won't mind putting together this quick casserole.

1 (7-oz.) pkg. elbow macaroni
Water
2 (6-1/2-oz.) cans tuna fish,
   drained and flaked
1 (10-3/4-oz.) can condensed
   cream of mushroom soup
1/2 cup plain yogurt, room temperature

1/2 cup sliced ripe olives
1/4 cup chopped green pepper
1/2 cup grated Cheddar cheese (2 oz.)
1 tablespoon instant minced onion
1/2 teaspoon salt
1 (17-oz.) can peas, drained
Sliced black olives for garnish

Preheat oven to 350°F (175°C). Generously butter a 1-1/2-quart casserole. Set aside. Cook macaroni in water according to package directions. Drain. In a large bowl, mix macaroni, tuna fish, soup, yogurt, olives, green pepper, half the cheese, minced onion and salt. Fold in peas. Put in prepared casserole. Sprinkle with remaining cheese. Bake 25 to 30 minutes until cheese is golden brown. Garnish with sliced black olives. Serve hot. Makes about 6 servings.

Ratatouille

Something extra special for vegetable lovers.

2 medium zucchini, thinly sliced
2 medium eggplants, peeled and sliced
5 tablespoons vegetable oil
1 small onion, sliced lengthwise
2 cups cooked long-grain rice
2 large tomatoes, thinly sliced

1 chicken bouillon cube, if desired
1/2 cup boiling water
1 teaspoon sugar
1 teaspoon dill weed
Quick Yogurt Glaze, page 103

Place zucchini and eggplant on 2 large baking sheets. Drizzle 2 tablespoons of the oil over vegetables on each baking sheet. Broil until golden brown on each side. Heat 1 tablespoon oil in a small skillet. Sauté onion until golden. In a 9-inch square baking pan, layer eggplant, zucchini, rice, tomatoes and onion. Dissolve bouillion cube in boiling water; add sugar and dill weed. Pour over vegetables. Preheat oven to 350°F (175°C). Bake about 20 minutes until golden brown. Prepare Yogurt Glaze. Spread over top of vegetables. Bake 30 more minutes until glaze is set. If desired, place glaze under broiler about 1 minute until lightly browned. Makes 6 to 8 servings.

Zucchini Casserole

Yogurt brings out all the subtle vegetable flavors.

1 cup water
4 medium zucchini, cubed
1 teaspoon salt
4 tablespoons butter or margarine
1-3/4 cups grated carrots
1/2 cup grated onion

1/2 cup plain yogurt, room temperature
1 (10-oz.) can cream of chicken soup
1 cup herb-seasoned croutons
2 tablespoons butter or margarine
1/2 cup herb-seasoned croutons

Preheat oven to 350°F (175°C). Butter a 2-quart casserole. Set aside. Bring water to a boil in a medium saucepan. Add zucchini and salt. Cover and cook about 10 minutes until tender. Drain well. In a medium skillet, melt 4 tablespoons butter or margarine. Sauté carrots and onion about 7 minutes. In a large bowl, stir yogurt until creamy. Add soup, cooked zucchini, carrot-onion mixture and 1 cup croutons. Gently mix all ingredients. Put in prepared casserole. Melt 2 tablespoons butter or margarine in a small skillet. Add 1/2 cup croutons. Toss to coat. Sprinkle over casserole. Bake 30 minutes until golden brown. Makes about 6 servings.

Variation

Substitute Italian beans, broccoli or a vegetable medley for zucchini.

Rice & Zucchini Casserole

Vegetable fans will love this unique rice.

2 lbs. zucchini	3 tablespoons tomato sauce
2 tablespoons vegetable oil	1/2 teaspoon dill weed
2 medium onions, chopped	1 teaspoon salt
1/4 cup uncooked long-grain rice	1/8 teaspoon pepper
1-1/2 cups water	1 cup plain yogurt, room temperature

Cut zucchini in half lengthwise, then in quarters. Heat oil in a 2-quart saucepan. Sauté onions until golden. Add rice, water, tomato sauce, dill weed, salt and pepper. Cover and cook about 15 minutes until rice is half done. Place half the zucchini quarters in a large skillet. Spread half the rice mixture evenly over zucchini. Layer remaining zucchini. Top with remaining rice mixture. Cover and cook 15 to 20 minutes zucchini is tender. Stir yogurt until creamy. Spoon over zucchini and rice just before serving. Makes about 6 servings.

Variation

Substitute eggplant, green beans or carrots for zucchini.

Continental Stuffed Vegetables

Delectable rice in its own vegetable cups.

2 small (6- to 7-inch) zucchini	1 small tomato, seeded and chopped
2 large green peppers, cut in half lengthwise	2 tablespoons minced parsley
	1/2 teaspoon dill weed
1/3 cup vegetable oil	1 teaspoon salt
2 tablespoons water	1/8 teaspoon pepper
1 medium onion, chopped	Dash garlic powder
1/2 cup uncooked long-grain rice	1/2 cup plain yogurt, room temperature
1 cup water	Plain yogurt, for garnish

Preheat oven to 350°F (175°C). Cut zucchini in half. Scoop out centers. Place in an 11" x 7" baking pan. Add green pepper halves. Add 2 tablespoons of the oil and 2 tablespoons water. Cover and bake 30 to 35 minutes. Heat remaining oil in a medium saucepan. Sauté onion until golden. Add rice, 1 cup water, tomato, parsley, dill weed, salt, pepper and garlic powder. Cover and cook 30 minutes until rice is tender. Remove from heat. Stir 1/2 cup yogurt until creamy. Carefully fold into rice mixture. Fill baked green pepper and zucchini halves with rice mixture. Top with yogurt. Makes about 4 servings.

Cauliflower Casserole

Shrimp and pecans transform cauliflower.

1 medium head cauliflower	1/2 cup milk
Boiling water	1 tablespoon flour
1 teaspoon salt	2 tablespoon butter or margarine, melted
1 cup plain yogurt, room temperature	1/4 cup chopped pecans
1 (10-oz.) can cream of shrimp soup	

Preheat oven to 350°F (175°C). Generously butter a 2-1/2-quart casserole. Set aside. Put cauliflower in a 2-quart saucepan. Add a small amount of boiling water and salt. Cover and cook about 20 minutes. Drain. Cut into flowerets. In a medium bowl, stir yogurt until creamy. Fold in soup. Stir in milk and flour. Drizzle butter or margarine into yogurt-soup mixture, stirring constantly. Arrange cauliflowerets in prepared casserole. Pour yogurt-soup mixture over cauliflower. Sprinkle pecans over casserole. Bake about 25 minutes until heated through. Makes about 6 servings.

Creamy Yogurt Sauce

A delicate white sauce for vegetables and fish.

2 tablespoons butter or margarine	1/2 teaspoon salt
2 tablespoons flour	Dash white pepper
1/2 cup milk	Pinch nutmeg, if desired
1 cup plain yogurt	

Melt butter or margarine in a small saucepan over low heat. Add flour. Cook and stir about 3 minutes. Stir in milk. Cook over low heat, stirring until thick and smooth. Stir yogurt until creamy. Slowly blend into sauce, stirring constantly. Stir in salt and white pepper. Add nutmeg, if desired. Serve over hot cooked vegetables or fish. Sauce may be stored in refrigerator up to 1 week. Makes about 1-1/2 cups.

Variations
Cheese Sauce: Stir in 1/2 teaspoon Worcestershire sauce and 1/2 cup grated Cheddar or American cheese. Heat over low heat until cheese melts.
Mushroom Sauce: Stir in 1 cup sautéed sliced fresh mushrooms and 1/2 teaspoon Worcestershire sauce. Heat to serving temperature. Serve over hot cooked vegetables such as green beans, spinach or broccoli.

Hollandaise Sauce

Serve this shortcut hollandaise over broccoli, asparagus or other green vegetables.

1/2 cup butter or margarine	3 tablespoons plain yogurt
3 egg yolks	Dash white pepper

Put butter or margarine, egg yolks and yogurt in a 1-quart saucepan. Let stand at room temperature at least 1/2 hour. Just before serving, cook over low heat 3 to 4 minutes, stirring until mixture thickens. Stir in white pepper. Serve at once over hot cooked broccoli or asparagus. To keep sauce warm, place dish of sauce in a pan of water the same temperature as the sauce. Makes about 3/4 cup.

How To Make Hollandaise Sauce

1/Half an hour before serving, place butter or margarine, egg yolks and yogurt in 1-quart saucepan.

2/Immediately after cooking, serve hot sauce over cooked broccoli.

Whipped Mashed Potatoes

Goes good with roast beef or steak.

6 medium boiling potatoes
Boiling water
1 teaspoon salt
1/2 cup plain yogurt, room temperature

4 tablespoons butter or margarine, softened
1/2 teaspoon salt
Dash white pepper

Wash and peel potatoes. Cut into cubes. Place in a 2-quart saucepan. Add a small amount of boiling water. Add 1 teaspoon salt. Cover and cook 10 to 15 minutes until tender. Drain. Gently shake pan over low heat to remove excess moisture. Mash potatoes. Stir yogurt until creamy. Add yogurt, butter or margarine, 1/2 teaspoon salt and white pepper to potatoes. With an electric mixer on low speed, whip until light and fluffy. Makes 4 to 6 servings.

Potato Strata

Simply sensational!

1 (5-oz.) pkg. scalloped potatoes
   with sauce mix
2 cups boiling water
3 tablespoons butter or margarine

1/2 cup shredded Cheddar cheese (2 oz.)
1/2 cup plain yogurt, room temperature
1 teaspoon cornstarch
1 egg

Preheat oven to 400°F (205°C). Place potatoes in an 11" x 7" baking pan. Sprinkle with sauce mix. Stir in boiling water and butter or margarine. Bake uncovered 35 to 45 minutes. Remove from oven. Reduce oven temperature to 350°F (175°C). Sprinkle cheese over potatoes. In a small bowl, stir yogurt and cornstarch until smooth and creamy. Beat in egg. Spread over cheese. Bake uncovered 10 more minutes until potatoes are tender. Cool 10 minutes before serving. Makes about 6 servings.

Spoon creamy plain yogurt on top of fried zucchini or eggplant.

Herb-Stuffed Baked Potatoes

Try this with next Sunday's roast.

6 medium baking potatoes
1/2 cup butter or margarine, softened
1 cup plain yogurt, room temperature
3/4 teaspoon rosemary
3/4 teaspoon parsley flakes

1/8 teaspoon sage
3/4 teaspoon salt
Dash white pepper
1 tablespoon butter or margarine, melted
Minced parsley, for garnish

Preheat oven to 350°F (175°C). Wash and dry potatoes. Pierce in several places with a fork. Bake 1 hour until tender. Remove from oven. Cut slice from top. Scoop out potatoes. Set shells aside. Mash potatoes. Add 1/2 cup soft butter or margarine. With an electric mixer on low speed, beat until creamy. Add yogurt, rosemary, parsley, sage, salt and white pepper. Beat again until creamy and fluffy. Fill potato shells. Brush lightly with melted butter. Place in a shallow baking pan. Increase oven temperature to 400°F (205°C). Bake 15 minutes until lightly browned. Sprinkle with parsley. Makes about 6 servings.

Baked Potato Topper

You may never go back to sour cream!

1 cup plain yogurt
1 teaspoon vegetable oil
1/2 teaspoon dill weed
1 tablespoon snipped chives

1/4 teaspoon salt
Dash white pepper
Crumbled cooked bacon, if desired

In a small bowl, stir yogurt until creamy. Drizzle oil into yogurt, stirring constantly. Add dill weed, chives, salt and pepper. Mix well. Serve over hot baked potatoes. Top with bacon, if desired. Makes about 1/2 cup, enough for 4 medium potatoes.

Bavarian Spaetzle

Tiny dumplings go with Veal Viennese, page 75 or Chicken Paprikash, page 79.

1 cup plain yogurt
2 eggs, slightly beaten
1/2 teaspoon salt
3-1/4 cups all-purpose flour,
   more if necessary

1/2 teaspoon baking soda
2 quarts chicken broth
1 teaspoon salt

In a large bowl, stir yogurt until creamy. Add beaten eggs, 1/2 teaspoon salt, flour and baking soda. Beat dough until thick and smooth. Add more flour if necessary. In a large saucepan, bring broth and 1 teaspoon salt to boil. Place 1/4 of dough on a wet chopping board. With hands flatten dough to 1/4-inch thickness. With a sharp knife, cut 1/4" x 2-1/2" strips. Slip strips off the chopping board 1 at a time directly into boiling broth. Repeat with remaining dough. Do not crowd into the broth. Dumplings should float when done. Remove with a slotted spoon. Rinse in hot water and keep warm. Makes 4 to 6 servings.

Fluffy Buttered Rice

Yogurt makes it extra good.

1-1/4 cups water
1 cup chicken broth
1 cup uncooked long-grain rice
1/2 teaspoon sugar

1/2 teaspoon salt
1/2 teaspoon lemon juice
4 tablespoons butter or margarine
Plain yogurt for topping

Preheat oven to 350°F (175°C). Bring water and broth to a boil in a 1-1/2-quart casserole. Add rice, sugar, salt and lemon juice. Bring to a boil again. Remove from heat. Cover and bake 25 to 30 minutes. Melt and lightly brown butter or margarine in a small skillet. Pour over hot cooked rice. Place a double thickness of paper towels on top of uncovered casserole to absorb extra moisture. Cover until serving time. Spoon a heaping tablespoon of yogurt over each serving. Makes about 6 servings.

Rice & Garbanzos

Latin America meets the Middle East.

1 cup uncooked long-grain rice
1/4 cup butter or margarine
1 teaspoon salt

2-1/2 cups boiling water
1 (15-oz.) can garbanzo beans, drained
1/2 cup plain yogurt, room temperature

In a medium saucepan over medium heat, sauté rice with butter or margarine and salt 3 to 5 minutes, stirring occasionally. Pour in boiling water. Add garbanzo beans. Cover and cook 20 to 25 minutes. Remove from heat. Stir yogurt until creamy. Gently fold into rice. Serve immediately. Makes about 8 servings.

Noodles a la Yogurt

Deliciously different.

1 (8-oz.) pkg. noodles, cooked and drained
6 tablespoons butter or margarine

1/3 cup plain yogurt, room temperature
Grated Parmesan cheese

Place cooked noodles in a warm serving bowl. Melt and lightly brown butter or margarine in a small skillet. Pour over noodles and toss gently to coat. Stir yogurt until creamy. Pour over noodles and toss gently. Sprinkle with cheese. Serve immediately. Makes about 6 to 8 servings.

All-Purpose Topping

A marvelous topping for fried eggplant, fish and more.

1/2 cup plain yogurt
2 teaspoons vegetable oil
2 tablespoons minced parsley
2 tablespoons grated onion

1/8 teaspoon garlic powder
1/8 teaspoon salt
Dash white pepper

In a small bowl, stir yogurt until creamy. Slowly drizzle oil into yogurt, stirring constantly. Add parsley, onion, garlic powder, salt and pepper. Mix well. Serve as a topping for fried eggplant, zucchini or fish. Makes about 1/2 cup.

Quick Yogurt Glaze

An ideal topping for a vegetable or meat casserole.

1 cup plain yogurt, room temperature
1 egg, slightly beaten

1 teaspoon cornstarch
2 tablespoons water

In a small bowl, stir yogurt until creamy. Slowly beat in egg. Mix cornstarch and water together. Blend into yogurt mixture. Spoon over a vegetable or meat casserole during last 20 minutes of baking. Bake until glaze is set. Makes about 1 cup.

How To Make Quick Yogurt Glaze

1/Mix cornstarch and water together. Blend into yogurt-egg mixture with a whisk.

2/Spoon sauce over a vegetable or meat casserole during the last 20 minutes of baking and continue baking until glaze is set.

Fish & Seafood

The tang of yogurt accents the delicate flavor in fish or seafood and makes it fun and easy to add fish to your menu.

Cooking time for fish is shorter than for meat. Overcooking fish spoils the flavor and texture. To test for doneness, gently probe a fork into the thickest part of the fish. The fish is done when the flesh separates and is tender and flaky. The separation made by the fork can be pushed together and brushed over with some sauce or butter.

One of the most popular ways to prepare fish is to dip it in batter and deep-fry it. I was amazed at the results of fish fillets dipped in yogurt batter! Golden Fried Fish is crisp, puffy and beautiful!

Broiled Salmon Steaks are brushed with a yogurt topping before broiling. It enhances the flavor. One of my favorites is Golden Puff Fillets. A yogurt-tartar sauce is spread over the tops during the last few minutes of cooking. It's beautiful!

I added yogurt to my favorite sauces and came up with a yogurt version of Creole Sauce, Oregano Sauce, Dill Sauce and Kicky Tartar Sauce.

Put fish and yogurt on tonight's menu and enjoy the wonderful flavor!

FISHERMAN'S NET
Shrimp-Stuffed Flounder, page 108
Parsley Potatoes
Glazed Carrots
Cucumber Salad
Lemon Cookies
Tea

ADMIRAL'S PLEASURE
Chilled Tomato Juice
Seafood Newburg, page 105
Leafy Green Salad Bowl
Croissants
Butter Curls
Frosty Lemon Fluff, page 144
Coffee

FRIDAY'S FISH FRY
Golden Fried Fish, page 105
Kicky Tartar Sauce, page 113
Cole Slaw
French Fries
Lime Sherbet
Lemonade

THE LIGHTHOUSE
Supreme Salmon Loaf, page 106
Hash Brown Potatoes
Peas
Spinach Salad
Hot Bacon Dressing
Poppy Seed Hard Rolls
Fruit Medley
Tea

Seafood Newburg

An elegant casserole.

1/2 cup butter or margarine	1/2 teaspoon Worcestershire sauce
1/2 lb. fresh mushrooms, sliced	1 tablespoon dry sherry wine
1/4 cup all-purpose flour	1 lb. shelled shrimp, cooked
1 teaspoon salt	1 (6-1/2-oz.) can crabmeat,
Dash white pepper	drained and flaked
1/4 teaspoon paprika	1 lb. fresh uncooked scallops
2 cups milk	2 hard-cooked eggs, sliced
1 cup plain yogurt, room temperature	1/3 cup sliced pimiento-stuffed olives
2 egg yolks	1 cup crushed potato chips

Preheat oven to 325°F (165°C). Melt butter or margarine in a medium saucepan. Add mushrooms. Cook 5 minutes. Remove mushrooms from pan. Stir in flour, salt, white pepper and paprika. Cook over low heat until bubbly. Add milk. Cook about 5 minutes, stirring constantly until thickened. Simmer 10 minutes. In a small bowl, stir yogurt until creamy. Blend in egg yolks. Blend a small amount of sauce into yogurt-egg mixture. Gradually add yogurt-sauce mixture to remaining sauce. Cook 5 minutes. Remove from heat. Add Worcestershire sauce, wine and sautéed mushrooms. Cut shrimp in half lengthwise. Place half the shrimp, half the crabmeat and half the scallops in an 11" x 7" baking pan. Arrange sliced eggs on top. Sprinkle with olive slices. Cover with half the sauce. Layer with remaining shrimp, crabmeat and scallops. Top with remaining sauce. Sprinkle with crushed potato chips. Bake about 30 minutes until lightly browned. Makes about 8 servings.

Golden Fried Fish

A winner at any fish fry.

1 lb. haddock, cod or perch fillets,	1/2 teaspoon baking powder
fresh or frozen	1/2 teaspoon baking soda
1 cup plain yogurt, room temperature	1 tablespoon vegetable oil
1 cup all-purpose flour	2 eggs, slightly beaten
1 tablespoon salt	Oil for deep-fat frying

Thaw fish, if frozen. Pat dry with paper towels. In a medium bowl, stir yogurt until creamy. Stir flour, salt, baking powder and baking soda into yogurt. Stir to blend. Add oil and eggs. Stir until batter is light and frothy. Stir batter occasionally to keep it mixed well. Heat oil to 375°F (190°C). Dip fillets into batter. Fry about 2 minutes on each side until golden brown. Drain on paper towels. Serve warm. Makes about 3 to 4 servings.

Broiled Salmon Steaks

Brush steaks with yogurt and serve with a tasty sauce.

4 salmon steaks, 1-inch thick
1/4 cup plain yogurt
1 tablespoon vegetable oil
1/2 teaspoon salt

Dash pepper
Dill Sauce, page 113
Snipped chives

Fasten salmon steak tips with wooden picks. In a small bowl, stir yogurt until creamy. Drizzle oil into yogurt, blending well. Stir in salt and pepper. Place steaks on broiler pan. Brush with yogurt mixture. Broil 3 to 4 inches from low heat about 20 to 25 minutes. Do not turn. Place on a warm platter. Spoon Dill Sauce over steaks. Sprinkle with chives. Makes about 8 servings.

Supreme Salmon Loaf

Dress up salmon with a snappy sauce.

1 (1-lb.) can salmon
2/3 cup plain yogurt, room temperature
1 cup coarsely crumbled cracker crumbs
1 egg

1 tablespoon instant minced onion
1 teaspoon salt
Dash pepper
Olive Sauce, see below

Olive Sauce:

1 cup plain yogurt, room temperature
8 black olives, chopped

2 small sweet pickles, chopped
2 green onions, thinly sliced

Preheat oven to 350°F (175°C). Butter a 7" x 3" loaf pan. Set aside. Drain salmon and remove skin. Remove all bones. In a large bowl, stir yogurt until creamy. Soak cracker crumbs in yogurt. Stir in egg. Add onion, salmon, salt and pepper. Mix well. Put in prepared pan. Bake about 30 minutes until golden brown. Prepare Olive Sauce. Serve over hot salmon loaf. Makes about 4 servings.

Olive Sauce:
In a small bowl, stir yogurt until creamy. Fold in olives, pickles and onions. Refrigerate while loaf is baking.

Shrimp-Stuffed Flounder

Half the shrimp goes in the stuffing and half goes in the sauce.

6 (1-1/2-lb.) flounder fillets or sole,
  fresh or frozen
1/2 teaspoon salt
1/8 teaspoon pepper
2 tablespoons butter or margarine
2 tablespoons grated onion
1/8 teaspoon tarragon
1/2 (4-1/2-oz.) can shrimp, drained

1/4 cup fine dry breadcrumbs
1 egg, slightly beaten
2 tablespoons butter or margarine,
  softened
2 tablespoons lemon juice
Paprika, for garnish
Shrimp Sauce

Shrimp Sauce:

2 tablespoons butter or margarine
2 tablespoons flour
2 tablespoons dry white wine
1 cup plain yogurt, room temperature

1/4 teaspoon salt
Dash white pepper
1/8 teaspoon tarragon
1/2 (4-1/2-oz.) can shrimp, minced

Thaw fish, if frozen. Pat dry with paper towels. Preheat oven to 350°F (175°C). Generously butter an 11" x 7" baking pan. Sprinkle flounder with salt and pepper. Let stand in a colander 10 minutes. Melt 2 tablespoons butter or margarine in a small skillet. Sauté onion and tarragon until onion is golden. Add half the shrimp. Heat well. Remove from heat. Stir in breadcrumbs and beaten egg. In a small bowl, mix 2 tablespoons butter or margarine and lemon juice. Brush on both sides of fillets. Place 1/4 cup shrimp mixture on each fillet and fold over. Place in prepared pan. Bake about 20 minutes until fish flakes easily when tested with a fork. Prepare Shrimp Sauce. Serve over stuffed flounder. Sprinkle with paprika. Makes about 3 to 4 servings.

Shrimp Sauce:

Melt butter or margarine in small skillet. Add flour. Stir in wine. Cook and stir 3 to 5 minutes. Stir yogurt until creamy. Gradually stir into flour mixture. Add salt, pepper and tarragon. Fold in shrimp. Heat to serving temperature. Serve immediately.

Variation

Use Shrimp Sauce over hot cooked cauliflower or any broiled fish.

For a quick tartar sauce, combine 1 cup plain yogurt with 1/2 cup drained sweet pickle relish. To make another quick and delicious sauce for fish or seafood, combine 1/2 cup yogurt and 1/2 cup seafood cocktail sauce. Chill before serving.

Crab-Rice Cakes

Horseradish sauce brings out the flavor.

2 tablespoons butter or margarine
2 tablespoons all-purpose flour
1/2 cup plain yogurt, room temperature
1 egg
2 tablespoons lemon juice
1/8 teaspoon pepper
2/3 cup chopped pimiento-stuffed olives
1/4 cup minced onion

1-1/2 cups cooked rice
1 (6-1/2-oz.) can crabmeat, drained
  and flaked
3 cups fine cornflake crumbs
1 egg
1/3 cup milk
Oil for deep-fat frying
Horseradish Sauce, page 114

Melt butter or margarine in a 1-quart saucepan. Blend in flour. Cook 1 minute. Stir yogurt until creamy. Blend yogurt into butter-flour mixture. Simmer over low heat 1 minute, stirring. Remove from heat. In a large bowl, beat 1 egg. Gradually blend in flour mixture. Stir in lemon juice, pepper, olives, onion, cooked rice, crabmeat and 1/2 cup of the cornflake crumbs. Mix well. Cover and refrigerate 1 hour. Using about 1/4 cup mixture for each cake, shape into 3-inch flat cakes. Beat remaining egg with milk. Dip cakes into egg-milk mixture, then into remaining cornflake crumbs. Heat oil to 375°F (190°C). Fry cakes about 2 to 3 minutes until golden brown. Drain on paper towels. Keep warm. Serve with Horseradish Sauce. Makes about 9 cakes.

Variation
Substitute 1 (6-1/2-oz.) can tuna, drained and flaked, or 1 (6-1/2-oz.) can minced clams for the crabmeat.

How To Make Shrimp-Stuffed Flounder

1/To make filling, sauté shrimp with onion and tarragon and remove from heat before stirring in breadcrumbs and beaten egg.

2/Brush fillets with butter-lemon mixture before filling. Fold fillets over filling and bake in a buttered baking pan.

Crab Louis

Only a few minutes of preparation in the morning and lunch is ready at noon.

2 (6-1/2-oz.) cans crabmeat
Seafood Dressing, see below
2 tomatoes
1 small head lettuce

1 head Bibb lettuce
Black olives, for garnish
Paprika, for garnish
Watercress, for garnish

Seafood Dressing:
1 cup plain yogurt
6 tablespoons seafood cocktail sauce
1/4 cup mayonnaise-style salad dressing
  (not mayonnaise)
1/4 cup minced celery

2 tablespoons minced green pepper
2 tablespoons minced green onion
1/4 teaspoon salt
Dash white pepper

Drain crabmeat. Remove bits of shell or cartilage. Leave crabmeat in chunks. Refrigerate 1 to 2 hours. Prepare Seafood Dressing. Cut tomatoes into wedges. Place large lettuce leaves on 4 individual plates. Shred remaining lettuce and Bibb lettuce. Arrange on lettuce leaves. Place crabmeat on shredded lettuce. Garnish with tomato wedges and black olives. Pour 1/4 cup Seafood Dressing over each salad. Sprinkle with paprika and garnish with watercress. Pass remaining dressing. Makes about 4 servings.

Seafood Dressing:
In a medium bowl, stir yogurt until creamy. Add cocktail sauce, salad dressing, celery, green pepper, onion, salt and white pepper. Refrigerate 1 hour.

Golden Puff Fillets

Something special from the galley.

1 lb. cod, haddock, flounder or perch,
  fresh or frozen
Salt and pepper to taste
2 tablespoons butter or margarine, melted
1/4 cup plain yogurt, room temperature

1 tablespoon vegetable oil
1 tablespoon sweet pickle relish,
  well-drained
1/2 teaspoon grated onion
1 egg white

Thaw fish, if frozen. Pat dry with paper towels. Generously butter a shallow baking pan. Place fish skin-side down in pan. Season with salt and pepper. Brush with butter or margarine. Broil 4 inches from medium heat about 10 to 15 minutes. While fish is broiling, stir yogurt until creamy in a small bowl. Drizzle oil into yogurt, stirring constantly. Blend in pickle relish and onion. In a small bowl, beat egg white until stiff. Gently fold yogurt mixture into beaten egg white. Spread over fish during last 2 minutes of broiling. Broil until fish is golden and flakes easily when tested with a fork. Makes about 3 servings.

Crab Mousse

An impressive dish to set before your crew.

2 envelopes unflavored gelatin
3/4 cup water
1/4 cup dry white wine
2 cups lemon-flavored yogurt
3 tablespoons mayonnaise-style salad dressing
   (not mayonnaise)
1 tablespoon grated onion

1 teaspoon salt
1/4 teaspoon white pepper
2 (6-oz.) pkgs. frozen crabmeat,
   thawed, drained and flaked
1 cup minced celery
2 tablespoons minced parsley

Generously oil a 6-cup mold. Mix gelatin and water in a medium saucepan. Stir over low heat to dissolve gelatin. Add wine, yogurt, salad dressing, onion, salt and white pepper. Mix well with an electric mixer or blender. Refrigerate until partially set. Fold in crabmeat, celery and parsley. Spoon into prepared mold. Refrigerate about 5 hours until firm. Invert to unmold. Makes about 6 servings.

How To Make Crab Mousse

1/Refrigerate yogurt-gelatin mixture until partially set before folding in crabmeat, celery and parsley.

2/Spoon crab mousse mixture into a generously oiled mold. Oiling the mold makes it easier to unmold set gelatin.

Codfish Cocktail

Surprise everyone with this mock crab cocktail.

Cocktail Sauce, see below
1/4 cup water
3/4 lb. codfish
1 carrot, cut in 2-inch pieces
5 (2-inch) pieces celery

Dash salt
Shredded lettuce
Lemon wedges, for garnish
Paprika, for garnish

Cocktail Sauce:
1/2 cup plain yogurt
1 tablespoon vegetable oil
2 tablespoons seafood cocktail sauce
1 teaspoon lemon juice

1/2 teaspoon horseradish
1 teaspoon minced onion
3 drops Tabasco® sauce
1/2 teaspoon Worcestershire sauce

Prepare Cocktail Sauce. Bring water to a boil in a medium saucepan. Add codfish, carrot, celery and salt. Cover and cook gently about 10 minutes until codfish is tender and flakes easily when tested with a fork. Discard vegetables and drain codfish well. Refrigerate 1 to 2 hours. Line individual plates with shredded lettuce. Flake codfish and place on lettuce. Pour Cocktail Sauce over codfish. Garnish with lemon wedges and sprinkle with paprika. Makes about 6 servings.

Cocktail Sauce:
In a small bowl, stir yogurt until creamy. Slowly drizzle oil into yogurt, stirring constantly. Add remaining ingredients. Blend well. Refrigerate 3 hours.

Cauliflower-Shrimp Salad

A delightful low-calorie luncheon.

2 (4-1/2-oz.) cans shrimp
1 small head cauliflower
1 cup cooked long-grain rice
1/2 green pepper, minced
1 small onion, minced
12 pimiento-stuffed green olives, thinly sliced

Few drops Tabasco® sauce
1 cup lemon-flavored yogurt
Salt to taste
Lettuce cups
Tomato wedges for garnish
Black olives for garnish

Cut shrimp in half. Place in a medium bowl. Cut cauliflower buds off each floweret. Mince into small pieces about the size of a grain of rice. Add to shrimp. Mix in rice, green pepper, onion, green olives and Tabasco® sauce. Toss. Stir yogurt until creamy. Fold into salad. Add salt to taste. Refrigerate 1 hour before serving. Place lettuce cups on individual plates. Spoon salad into cups. Garnish with tomato wedges and black olives. Makes about 4 servings.

Kicky Tartar Sauce

Everyone will ask for more—make sure there's enough to go around.

1 cup plain yogurt
2 tablespoons vegetable oil
2 tablespoons sweet pickle relish,
   well drained
1 tablespoon instant minced onion

1 tablespoon minced parsley
1/8 teaspoon oregano
1/8 teaspoon salt
1/8 teaspoon garlic powder
1/8 teaspoon white pepper

In a small bowl, stir yogurt until creamy. Drizzle oil into yogurt, stirring constantly. Add pickle relish, onion, parsley, oregano, salt, garlic powder and white pepper. Mix well. Refrigerate 1 to 2 hours. Serve with deep-fried or broiled fish or seafood. Makes about 1 cup.

Almond Sauce

Especially good with fried perch, sole or red snapper.

3 tablespoons butter or margarine
1/3 cup blanched, slivered almonds
1 tablespoon minced onion
1/8 teaspoon minced garlic
1 teaspoon all-purpose flour

3 tablespoons dry white wine
3 tablespoons water
1/4 teaspoon salt
1/2 cup plain yogurt, room temperature

Melt butter or margarine in a medium saucepan. Add almonds, onion and garlic. Cook until onion is golden brown. Stir in flour. Add wine, water and salt. Cook until thickened. Remove from heat. Stir yogurt until creamy. Gradually blend into sauce. Serve with fried perch, sole or red snapper. Makes about 1-3/4 cups.

Dill Sauce

This delicate sauce doubles as a salad dressing.

1/2 cup plain yogurt
2 tablespoons vegetable oil
1 tablespoon vinegar

1 tablespoon minced onion
1 tablespoon minced parsley
1/2 teaspoon dill weed

In a small bowl, stir yogurt until creamy. Drizzle oil into yogurt, stirring constantly. Stir in vinegar, onion, parsley and dill weed. Refrigerate 1 to 2 hours. Serve with broiled or fried fish, broiled hamburgers or over tossed salad. Makes about 1/2 cup.

Creole Sauce

Down on the bayou they serve this sauce with fresh shrimp.

2 tablespoons vegetable oil
2 tablespoons grated onion
1/4 cup minced green pepper
1 (8-oz.) can stewed tomatoes
1/3 cup sliced pimiento-stuffed olives

1 tablespoon sherry
1/4 teaspoon salt
1/8 teaspoon pepper
1/2 cup plain yogurt, room temperature

Heat oil in a small saucepan. Add onion and green pepper. Sauté until onion is golden brown. Add tomatoes, olives, sherry, salt and pepper. Cook 2 to 3 minutes. Remove from heat. In a small bowl, stir yogurt until creamy. Blend a small amount of hot sauce into yogurt. Gradually add yogurt-sauce mixture to remaining sauce. Heat to serving temperature. Serve with fried perch or shrimp. Makes about 1-3/4 cups.

Oregano Sauce

Enhance broiled fish with this flavorful sauce.

1 cup plain yogurt
1/4 cup vegetable oil
3 tablespoons parsley
3 tablespoons minced onion

2 tablespoons lemon juice
1/2 teaspoon oregano
1/4 teaspoon salt
1/8 teaspoon pepper

In a small bowl, stir yogurt until creamy. Slowly drizzle oil into yogurt, stirring constantly. Add parsley, onion, lemon juice, oregano, salt and pepper. Refrigerate 1 to 2 hours. Serve with broiled fish. Makes about 1 cup.

Horseradish Sauce

Lots of pizzazz for fish or seafood.

1 cup plain yogurt
1 tablespoon vegetable oil
3 tablespoons horseradish, well-drained

1 tablespoon white vinegar
1/4 teaspoon salt
1/4 teaspoon white pepper

In a small bowl, stir yogurt until creamy. Drizzle oil into yogurt, stirring constantly. Add horseradish, vinegar, salt and white pepper. Mix well. Serve with broiled or fried fish or seafood. Makes about 1 cup sauce.

Breads

Because of today's interest in natural food, many of us are baking our own bread. Whether you are an expert baker or a beginner, you'll be proud to serve yogurt breads. In experimenting with yogurt in bread recipes, I created a bread similar in taste and texture to sourdough bread but without using sourdough starter. My family calls it Sophie Kay's Old-Fashioned Bread.

I also discovered that under the crisp, flaky crust, yogurt gave breads a velvety texture and delicate taste. So yogurt French Bread was born!

If this is your first bread-baking experience, try Easy Honey Rolls. It's easy beginning with yogurt added to packaged hot roll mix.

Beginners and seasoned bakers alike will have instant success and praise with easy-to-make Whole-Wheat Onion Bread and Dilly Onion Bread. For a special treat, spread Yogo-Cheese, page 161, on your own home-baked bread.

Remember, all ingredients should be at room temperature, including the yogurt. I used homemade yogurt in all the bread recipes. You can use Plain Yogurt, page 13, or Whole Milk Yogurt, page 14, or buy unflavored plain yogurt.

FAMILY DINNER
Broiled Steak
Sautéed Mushrooms
Baked Potatoes
Baked Potato Topper, page 100
French Beans Almondine
Dilly Onion Bread, page 116
Ice Cream
Coffee or Milk

SIMPLY ITALIAN
Antipasto
Spaghetti & Meatballs
Italian Salad
French Bread, page 118
Spumoni
Coffee

SNACKTIME
Giant Pretzels, page 123
Hot Mustard
Famous California Dip, page 37
Celery & Carrot Sticks
Fruit Drink

MIDWEST DINNER
Fried Chicken
Riced Potatoes
Broccoli Spears
Skillet Corn Bread, page 120
Apricot Tarts
Lemonade

Sophie Kay's Old-Fashioned Bread

You'll think it's sourdough bread.

5-1/2 to 6-1/2 cups all-purpose flour
2 pkgs. active dry yeast
2 tablespoons sugar
1-1/2 teaspoons salt

1 cup plain yogurt, room temperature
1 cup water
1 tablespoon shortening
1 tablespoon milk

Generously grease two 9" x 5" loaf pans. Set aside. In a large bowl, mix 2 cups flour, yeast, sugar and salt. In a 1-quart saucepan, stir yogurt until creamy. Add water and shortening. Heat until warm, about 120°F (50°C). Add yogurt mixture to flour mixture. Blend with an electric mixer on low speed until all ingredients are moistened. Beat 3 more minutes on medium speed. By hand, stir in enough remaining flour to make a firm dough. On a lightly floured surface, knead dough 5 to 10 minutes until smooth and elastic. Lightly butter bowl. Put dough in bowl and turn to butter top. Cover and let rise in warm place about 1 hour until doubled in bulk. Punch down dough. Cover and let rise again about 45 minutes until doubled in bulk. Punch down dough. Divide dough in half. On a lightly floured surface, roll out or pat each half to a 7" x 14" rectangle. Starting with short side, roll up tightly like a jelly roll, pressing dough down. Pinch edges and ends to seal. Place in prepared loaf pans. Cover and let rise about 30 minutes until doubled in bulk. Brush top with milk. Preheat oven to 400°F (205°C). Bake 30 to 40 minutes until golden brown. Remove from pans. Cool on wire racks. Makes 2 loaves.

Dilly Onion Bread

Yogurt, onion and dill flavor this tasty round loaf.

3 to 3-1/4 cups all-purpose flour
2 pkgs. active dry yeast
2 tablespoons sugar
1 tablespoon instant minced onion
1 teaspoon salt
2 teaspoons dill weed

1 cup plain yogurt, room temperature
1/4 cup water
2 tablespoons butter or margarine
2 eggs
About 1 teaspoon butter or margarine, melted

Generously grease a 2-quart round casserole. Set aside. In a large bowl, mix 1-1/2 cups of the flour, yeast, sugar, onion, salt and dill weed. In a 1-quart saucepan, stir yogurt until creamy. Add water and 2 tablespoons butter or margarine. Heat until warm, about 120°F (50°C). Butter or margarine does not need to melt. Add warm yogurt mixture and eggs to flour mixture. Blend with an electric mixer on low speed until all ingredients are moistened. Beat 3 more minutes on medium speed. By hand, stir in enough remaining flour to make a firm batter. Spoon into prepared casserole. Cover and let rise in a warm place 50 to 60 minutes until doubled in bulk. Preheat oven to 375°F (190°C). Bake 25 to 30 minutes until golden brown. Remove from casserole. Brush top with about 1 teaspoon melted butter or margarine. Cool on a wire rack. Serve warm or cold. Makes 1 loaf.

French Bread

Be sure to serve this with your next spaghetti dinner.

Yellow cornmeal
5 to 5-1/2 cups all-purpose flour
2 pkgs. active dry yeast
1 tablespoon sugar
2 teaspoons salt
1/2 teaspoon baking soda

1 cup plain yogurt, room temperature
1-1/2 cups warm water (120°F, 50°C)
3 tablespoons shortening
1 egg white
1 tablespoon water

Grease 2 baking sheets. Sprinkle with cornmeal and set aside. Lightly butter a large bowl to hold rising dough; set aside. In another large bowl, mix 1-1/2 cups of the flour, yeast, sugar, salt and baking soda. Stir yogurt until creamy. Add yogurt, warm water and shortening. Blend with an electric mixer on low speed until all ingredients are moistened. Beat 3 more minutes on medium speed. By hand, stir in enough remaining flour to make a slightly firm dough. On a lightly floured surface, knead dough 5 to 10 minutes until smooth and elastic. Put dough in buttered bowl. Turn to butter top. Cover and let rise in a warm place about 1 hour until doubled in bulk. Punch down dough. Divide dough in half. On a lightly floured surface, roll out or pat each half to a 9" x 18" rectangle. Starting with the long side, roll up tightly like a jelly roll, pressing dough down. Pinch edges and ends to seal. Fold ends under loaf. Place seam-side down on prepared baking sheet. With a sharp knife, make 3 diagonal slashes across top. Cover and let rise in warm place about 30 minutes until doubled in bulk. Repeat with remaining dough. Preheat oven to 400°F (205°C). Beat egg white and water together. Brush on top of loaves. Bake 35 to 50 minutes until golden brown. For a very crusty loaf, brush bread again with egg mixture during last 5 minutes of baking. Makes 2 loaves.

Irish Soda Bread

You can start this easy bread about an hour before dinner.

2 cups sifted all-purpose flour
1/2 teaspoon salt
3/4 teaspoon baking soda
1 tablespoon sugar
1/3 cup raisins

1 tablespoon caraway seeds
1/2 cup plain yogurt, room temperature
1/4 cup plus 2 tablespoons water
1 teaspoon milk

Preheat oven to 400°F (205°). Grease a baking sheet. Set aside. In a medium bowl, sift flour, salt, baking soda and sugar. Add raisins and caraway seeds. Mix well. In a small bowl, stir yogurt until creamy. Add water and blend well. Add to flour mixture. Mix to a smooth dough. On a lightly floured surface, knead dough 5 to 15 minutes until smooth and elastic. Shape into a ball. Place on baking sheet. With a scissors, cut a cross on top. Brush top with milk. Bake 35 to 40 minutes until lightly browned. Serve warm. Makes 1 loaf.

Whole-Wheat Onion Bread

A better blend of flavors is hard to find.

3 cups all-purpose flour
2-1/2 cups whole-wheat flour
2 pkgs. active dry yeast
2 teaspoons salt
1 cup plain yogurt, room temperature

1-1/4 cups water
1 envelope onion soup mix
1/4 cup honey
2 tablespoons shortening
About 1 teaspoon butter or margarine, melted

Generously grease a 2-quart round casserole. Set aside. Stir together both flours. In a large bowl, mix 1-1/2 cups of the flour mixture, yeast and salt. In a 1-quart saucepan, stir yogurt until creamy. Add water, onion soup mix, honey and shortening. Cook and stir over low heat until warm, about 120°F (50°C). Shortening does not need to melt. Add yogurt mixture to flour-yeast mixture. Blend with an electric mixer on low speed, scraping bowl occasionally until all ingredients are moistened. Add 3/4 cup dry flour mixture. Beat on high speed 2 minutes. By hand, stir in enough remaining dry flour mixture to make a soft dough. Cover and let rise in warm place about 1-1/2 hours until doubled in bulk. Stir dough down. Turn into prepared casserole. Brush with melted butter or margarine. Let rise about 30 minutes until doubled in bulk. Preheat oven to 350°F (175°C). Bake 60 minutes until golden brown. Remove from casserole. Brush top with melted butter. Cool on a wire rack. Makes 1 loaf.

My Favorite Corn Bread

Homemade corn bread turns a simple meal into a feast!

1 cup yellow cornmeal
1 cup all-purpose flour
2 tablespoons sugar
2-1/2 teaspoons baking powder
1/2 teaspoon baking soda

1/2 teaspoon salt
3/4 cup plain yogurt, room temperature
2 eggs, slightly beaten
1/4 cup water
1/4 cup vegetable oil

Preheat oven to 425°F (220°C). Generously grease an 8-inch square baking pan. Set aside. In a large bowl, mix cornmeal, flour, sugar, baking powder, baking soda and salt. Stir yogurt until creamy. Add yogurt, eggs, water and oil. With a rotary beater, beat about 1 minute until just smooth. Do not overbeat. Pour into prepared pan. Bake 20 to 25 minutes until golden brown. Cut into squares. Makes about 9 servings.

Variation
To make corn sticks or corn muffins, pour corn bread batter into hot greased corn stick pans or muffin cups. Reduce baking time to 15 to 20 minutes.

Skillet Corn Bread

Complete your campfire supper with this quick and easy bread.

1 cup packaged pancake mix
1 cup yellow cornmeal
1 teaspoon baking powder
1/2 teaspoon baking soda
1/2 teaspoon salt

1/2 cup plain yogurt, room temperature
1/2 cup water
2 eggs, slightly beaten
1 tablespoon vegetable oil
Butter or margarine, softened

Generously butter a 10-inch skillet. Set aside. In a large bowl, mix pancake mix, cornmeal, baking powder, baking soda and salt. Stir yogurt until creamy. Add yogurt, water, eggs and oil. With a rotary beater, beat about 1 minute until just smooth. Preheat buttered skillet over low heat 2 minutes. Pour corn bread mixture into warm skillet. Cook 10 to 12 minutes until top is almost set. With a spatula, loosen and turn over corn bread. Cook 10 more minutes until golden. Serve hot with soft butter or margarine. Makes 6 to 8 servings.

How To Make Skillet Corn Bread

1/Add yogurt, water, eggs and oil to pancake mix and corn-meal mixture. Beat until smooth before pouring into warm buttered skillet.

2/When top of cornbread is almost set, loosen edges with a spatula. Turn over and cook until golden.

Cloverleaf Dinner Rolls

Store these in your freezer and take them out as you need them.

2-1/2 to 3 cups all-purpose flour
1 pkg. active dry yeast
1/4 cup sugar
1/2 teaspoon salt
2 tablespoons warm water (110°F, 45°C)

1 cup plain yogurt, room temperature
1/2 cup butter or margarine, softened
1 egg
About 1/4 cup butter or margarine, melted

Set 1/2 cup flour aside for kneading. Lightly butter a large bowl to hold rising dough. Set aside. In another large bowl, dissolve yeast, sugar and salt in warm water. Stir yogurt until creamy. Slowly blend into yeast mixture. Blend in 1 cup flour. Add butter or margarine and egg. Mix well. By hand, stir in enough remaining flour to make a firm dough. Sprinkle reserved 1/2 cup flour on kneading surface. Knead dough 8 to 10 minutes until smooth and elastic. Place in buttered bowl. Turn dough to butter top. Cover and let rise in a warm place 1 to 1-1/2 hours until doubled in bulk. Generously grease muffin pans. Shape dough into 1-inch balls. Place 3 balls in each muffin cup. Brush with melted butter or margarine. Cover and let rise again in a warm place about 20 minutes until almost doubled in bulk. Preheat oven to 400°F (205°C). Bake 12 to 15 minutes until golden brown. Makes about 36 rolls.

Variation
To make Four-Leaf Clover Rolls, shape dough into 2-inch balls. Place 1 ball in each muffin cup. With scissors, cut each ball in half, then in quarters. Proceed as directed above. Makes about 48 rolls.

Easy Honey Rolls

If you're a beginner, start with these easy dinner rolls.

1 (13-3/4-oz.) pkg. hot roll mix
1/4 cup warm water (110°F, 45°C)
1/2 cup plain yogurt, room temperature
1 egg

1/4 cup honey
2 tablespoons butter or margarine, softened
1 egg white, slightly beaten

Generously grease 2 baking sheets. In a large bowl, dissolve yeast from hot roll mix in warm water. Stir yogurt until creamy. Add yogurt, egg, honey and butter or margarine. Add flour from hot roll mix. Blend well. Cover and let rise in warm place about 50 to 60 minutes until doubled in bulk. On a lightly floured surface, knead dough 1 or 2 minutes until smooth and elastic. Divide dough in half. Divide each half into 16 equal pieces. Form into desired shapes. To make Horseshoes, shape each piece of dough into a thin 7-inch roll. Form roll into a U shape. To make Figure 8's, shape each piece of dough into a thin 10-inch roll. Twist roll into a figure 8; seal ends. Place about 2 inches apart on prepared baking sheets. Cover and let rise in a warm place about 45 minutes until doubled in bulk. Preheat oven to 375°F (190°C). Brush tops lightly with beaten egg white. Bake about 15 minutes until golden brown. Remove from baking sheets. Cool on wire racks. Makes about 16 rolls.

Fancy Dinner Rolls

Adds an elegant touch to every meal.

6 to 6-1/2 cups all-purpose flour
2 pkgs. active dry yeast
2 tablespoons sugar
1 tablespoon salt
1/2 teaspoon baking soda
1 cup plain yogurt, room temperature

1-1/2 cups water
2 tablespoons shortening
1 egg, slightly beaten
1 tablespoon milk
Toasted sesame seeds, if desired
Poppy seeds, if desired

Generously grease 2 baking sheets. Lightly butter a large bowl to hold rising dough. In another large bowl, mix 2 cups of the flour, yeast, sugar, salt and baking soda. In a 1-quart saucepan stir yogurt until creamy. Add water and shortening. Heat until warm, about 120°F (50°C). Add yogurt mixture to flour mixture. Blend with an electric mixer on low speed until all ingredients are moistened. Beat 3 more minutes on medium speed. By hand, gradually add enough remaining flour to make a firm dough. On a lightly floured surface, knead dough 8 to 10 minutes until smooth and elastic. Put dough in buttered bowl. Turn to butter top. Cover and let rise in a warm place about 1 hour until doubled in bulk. Punch down dough. Divide dough in half. Divide each half into 18 equal pieces. Form into desired shapes. To make coils, shape each piece of dough into a thin 10-inch-long roll. Hold 1 end of roll and wind dough loosely around spiral-fashion. Tuck other end under. To make knots, shape each piece of dough into a thin 10-inch-long roll. Tie a loose knot. Place about 2 inches apart on prepared baking sheets. Cover and let rise in a warm place about 1 hour until doubled in bulk. Preheat oven to 400°F (205°C). Combine egg and milk. Brush lightly on rolls. If desired, sprinkle rolls with toasted sesame seeds or poppy seeds. Bake about 15 minutes until golden brown. Cool on wire racks. Makes about 36 rolls.

Basic Yogurt Biscuits

Old-fashioned taste with a new square shape.

2 cups all-purpose flour
1 tablespoon baking powder
1/4 teaspoon baking soda
1 teaspoon salt

1/4 cup shortening
3/4 cup plain yogurt, room temperature
About 1 teaspoon milk

Preheat oven to 450°F (220°C). In a large bowl, mix flour, baking powder, baking soda and salt. Cut in shortening until mixture resembles coarse crumbs. Stir yogurt until creamy. Add all at once to flour-shortening mixture. On a lightly floured surface, knead dough gently about 5 to 10 minutes until smooth. Roll out or pat to 1/2-inch thickness. With a knife cut dough into 2-inch squares. Place on ungreased baking sheet. Brush tops with milk. Bake about 12 to 15 minutes until lightly browned. Makes about 12 biscuits.

Variation
Add 1 tablespoon snipped chives with yogurt.

Dieter's Biscuits

Too good to be low-calorie—but they are!

2 cups sifted all-purpose flour
2 teaspoons baking powder
1/2 teaspoon baking soda

1/2 teaspoon salt
1 cup peach-flavored yogurt,
   room temperature

Preheat oven to 450°F (230°C). Grease a large baking sheet. Set aside. In a medium bowl, sift together flour, baking powder, baking soda and salt. Stir yogurt until creamy. Add to dry ingredients. Stir until just moistened. Drop by heaping tablespoons onto prepared baking sheet. Bake about 10 to 12 minutes until lightly browned. Makes about 24 biscuits.

Giant Pretzels

Delicious warm with a little hot mustard.

6-1/2 to 7-1/2 cups all-purpose flour
2 pkgs. active dry yeast
6 tablespoons sugar
1 tablespoon salt
1/2 teaspoon baking soda
1 cup plain yogurt, room temperature
1 cup water

3 tablespoons shortening
1 egg
1 egg yolk
2 tablespoons milk
Coarse salt
Prepared hot mustard

Lightly grease 2 baking sheets. Set aside. In a large bowl, mix 2 cups of the flour, yeast, sugar, salt and baking soda. In a 1-quart saucepan, stir yogurt until creamy. Add water and shortening. Heat until warm, about 120°F (50°C). Add yogurt mixture to flour mixture. Add egg. Blend with an electric mixer on low speed until all ingredients are moistened. Beat 3 more minutes on medium speed. By hand, gradually add enough remaining flour to make a firm dough. Cover bowl with aluminum foil. Refrigerate 4 hours or overnight. On a lightly floured surface, divide dough in half. Cut each half into 16 equal pieces. Roll each piece into a thin roll about 16 inches long. Bring ends together and twist around each other twice. Press twisted ends into center top of roll to form pretzel shape. Blend egg yolk and milk together. Brush pretzels with egg yolk mixture. Sprinkle with coarse salt. Let rise in a warm place about 25 minutes until doubled in bulk. Preheat oven to 425°F (220°C). Bake 15 to 20 minutes until golden brown. Cool on wire racks. Serve with hot mustard. Makes about 32 pretzels.

Variation
To make Salt Sticks, roll each piece of dough into a thin 6-inch length. Brush with egg yolk mixture and sprinkle with coarse salt. Let rise and bake as above.

Cakes & Cookies

Improve the flavor of cakes and cookies with yogurt. The rich chocolaty flavor of Devil's Food Cake is especially good. Its chocolate yogurt icing goes well on any chocolate or white cake. Dreamy Chocolate Cake has the subtle flavor of malted milk. After you've tried these 2 cakes, you'll know it's worth the effort to make them from scratch! Blue Ribbon Nut Cake, a winner at the Wisconsin State Fair, is sweet and moist with a delectable honey topping. Don't wait for a special occasion to make it.

Packaged mixes are popular and convenient. Try them with yogurt. The light texture of Quick & Easy Cake will fool everyone. When you add yogurt to instant vanilla pudding, Quick Boston Cream Pie is wonderful. But don't stop with vanilla! Add plain or flavored yogurt to other instant pudding mixes to use as fillings for pies and tortes.

Yogurt adds zest to cookies. My favorites are Peanut Butter Cookies Supreme, Chocolate Chip Bars and Oatmeal-Raisin Cookies. These cookies make it hard to keep your cookie jar full!

DINNER CALL
Broiled Lamb Chops
Minted Pineapple Garnish
Nifty Noodle Bake, page 91
Hollandaise Sauce, page 98
Dreamy Chocolate Cake, page 129
Milk

TEEN TIME
Hero Sandwich
Crisp Relishes
Sugar Monster Cookies, page 136
Chocolate Chip Bars, page 129
Yogurt Milkshake, page 39
Lemonade

DESSERT BRIDGE
Old-Fashioned Lemon Pound Cake, page 130
Coconut Frosted Ice Cream Balls
Mints
Nuts
Irish Coffee

CHRISTMAS SPIRIT
Plum Pudding
Fluffy Hard Sauce
Holiday Fruit Cake, page 130
Petit Fours
Spritz Cookies
Coffee & Punch

Quick & Easy Cake

If the cake mix you use calls for 1 cup water, use 2/3 cup yogurt and 1/3 cup water.

1 (18.5-oz.) pkg. yellow cake mix
2/3 cup plain yogurt
2/3 cup water

2 eggs
Fruit Icing, see below

Fruit Icing:
3 tablespoons butter
3-1/2 cups sifted powdered sugar
Grated peel of 1 lemon or orange

1 tablespoon lemon or orange juice
2-1/2 to 3 tablespoons plain yogurt

Preheat oven to 350°F (175°C). Generously grease and lightly flour two 9-inch round pans. Set aside. In a large bowl, blend cake mix, yogurt, water and eggs. Blend with an electric mixer on low speed, scraping bowl constantly until ingredients are moistened. Beat 4 minutes on medium speed, scraping bowl. Pour into prepared pans. Bake about 30 minutes. Cool in pans 10 minutes then remove and cool on wire racks. Prepare Fruit Icing and frost between layers and sides of cake. Makes one 2-layer cake.

Fruit Icing:
In a small bowl, cream butter. Stir in powdered sugar, lemon or orange peel, lemon juice and yogurt. Beat until smooth.

Variation
Substitute 1 pkg. white cake mix for the yellow cake mix. Substitute 2 egg whites for the whole eggs.

Whipped Yogurt Topping

A low-calorie substitute for whipped cream on pies and cakes.

1 cup Whipping Cream Yogurt, page 15
1 tablespoon powdered sugar

Chill a small bowl and beaters. Place yogurt in the chilled bowl. Beat with electric mixer on high speed about 4 minutes until thickened. Gradually add powdered sugar, beating well. Refrigerate about 3 hours until mixture is softly set, about the consistency of nondairy whipped topping. May be covered and stored in refrigerator up to 2 weeks. Makes about 1 cup, enough for one 9-inch cake or pie.

Citrus-Yogurt Cake

Everyone loves this delightful Greek cake!

Lemon Syrup, see below
6 eggs, separated
1/2 cup butter or margarine
3 tablespoons shortening
2 cups sugar
Grated peel of 1 orange

3 cups all-purpose flour
2 teaspoons baking powder
1 cup plain yogurt, room temperature
Whipped cream, for garnish
Mandarin orange or maraschino cherries,
  for garnish

Lemon Syrup:
1 cup sugar
1-1/2 cups water

1 teaspoon lemon juice

Prepare Lemon Syrup. Set aside to cool. Preheat oven to 350°F (175°C). Generously grease and lightly flour a 13" x 9" baking pan. Set aside. In a medium bowl, beat egg whites until stiff but not dry; set aside. In a large bowl, cream together butter or margarine, shortening and sugar. Add egg yolks 1 at a time, beating well after each. Add orange peel. In a medium bowl, sift together flour and baking powder. Stir yogurt until creamy. Add flour mixture alternately with yogurt to creamed mixture, beginning and ending with flour mixture. Gently fold beaten egg whites into batter. Pour into prepared pan. Bake about 40 to 45 minutes. Place pan on a wire rack. Spoon cooled syrup over hot cake, covering entire cake. Leave cake in pan to cool. Cut into 2-inch squares. Top with whipped cream and a wedge of mandarin orange or maraschino cherries. Makes about 24 pieces.

Lemon Syrup:
In a 1-quart saucepan, mix sugar, water and lemon juice. Bring to a boil over high heat. Reduce heat and boil gently 10 minutes.

Quick Lemon Frosting

Tangy and good.

1/2 cup lemon-flavored yogurt
2 cups sifted powdered sugar

In a small bowl, beat lemon-flavored yogurt and sifted powdered sugar. Mix well. Makes about 1 cup, enough to drizzle over two 9-inch cakes.

Devil's Food Cake

Surprisingly light and shamefully rich!

2 cups sifted cake flour
1-1/4 teaspoons baking soda
1/2 teaspoon salt
1/2 cup butter or margarine
1-1/4 cups sugar
2 eggs

2 (1-oz.) squares unsweetened chocolate,
   melted and cooled
1 teaspoon vanilla extract
3/4 cup plain yogurt, room temperature
1/3 cup boiling water
Fluffy Chocolate Icing, see below

Fluffy Chocolate Icing:
5 tablespoons butter
2 (1-oz.) squares unsweetened chocolate,
   melted and cooled
3 cups sifted powdered sugar

1/4 cup plain yogurt
1 egg yolk
1 teaspoon vanilla extract

Preheat oven to 375°F (190°C). Generously grease and lightly flour two 9-inch round baking pans. Set aside. Sift together cake flour, baking soda and salt. In a large bowl, cream butter or margarine. Add sugar and beat until light and fluffy. Add eggs 1 at a time, beating well after each. Stir in chocolate and vanilla extract. Stir yogurt until creamy. Add cake flour mixture alternately with yogurt, beginning and ending with cake flour mixture. Add boiling water. Mix well. Pour into prepared pans. Bake 25 to 30 minutes. When cold, spread Fluffy Chocolate Icing between layers and on top and sides. Makes one 2-layer cake.

Fluffy Chocolate Icing:
In a small bowl, cream butter. Add cooled melted chocolate. Mix well. Beat in sugar alternately with yogurt. Add egg yolk and vanilla extract. Beat until icing is light and fluffy. This is a good chocolate icing for other cakes too.

Quick Chocolate Frosting

Unexpected guests? They'll like this quick frosting.

1 (6-oz.) pkg. semisweet
   chocolate chips (1 cup)

1/4 cup plain yogurt, room temperature

Melt chocolate chips in a double boiler over boiling water. Remove from heat. Stir yogurt until creamy. Gradually blend yogurt into chocolate. Makes about 1 cup, enough for 1 single layer cake.

Dreamy Chocolate Cake

Tastes like malted milk!

4 oz. chocolate chips (2/3 cup)
1/2 cup boiling water
4 eggs, separated
2-1/2 cups sifted cake flour
1 teaspoon baking soda
1/2 teaspoon salt

1 cup butter or margarine
2 cups sugar
1 teaspoon vanilla extract
1 cup plain yogurt, room temperature
Coconut Pecan Frosting, see below

Coconut Pecan Frosting:
1 cup evaporated milk
1 cup sugar
3 egg yolks
1/2 cup butter or margarine

1 teaspoon vanilla extract
1 (4-oz.) can flaked coconut
1 cup chopped pecans

Preheat oven to 350°F (175°C). Generously grease and lightly flour three 9-inch round pans. Set aside. Melt chocolate chips in boiling water. Set aside to cool. In a small bowl, beat egg whites until stiff; set aside. In a medium bowl, sift together cake flour, baking soda and salt. In a large bowl, cream butter or margarine. Gradually add sugar, beating until light and fluffy. Add egg yolks 1 at a time, beating well after each. Stir in chocolate and vanilla extract. Mix well. Add cake flour mixture alternately with yogurt, beginning and ending with cake flour mixture. Gently fold beaten egg whites into batter. Pour into prepared pans. Bake 30 to 35 minutes. Cool 10 minutes in pans, then remove and cool on wire racks. Prepare Coconut Pecan Frosting. Frost cake between layers and on top. Makes one 3-layer cake.

Coconut Pecan Frosting:
In a small saucepan, combine evaporated milk, sugar, egg yolks and butter or margarine. Cook and stir until mixture thickens, about 12 minutes. Remove from heat. Stir in vanilla extract, coconut and pecans. Beat until mixture is cool and reaches spreading consistency.

Chocolate Chip Bars

When snacktime comes around, have the cookie jar full of these.

1 (1-lb.) pkg. chocolate chip cookie mix
1/4 lb. butter or margarine, softened
1/2 cup plain yogurt, room temperature

1/2 cup coconut
1/2 cup chopped nuts
1 teaspoon vanilla extract

Preheat oven to 350°F (175°C). Generously grease a 13" x 9" baking pan. Put chocolate chip mix in a large bowl. Add butter or margarine, yogurt, coconut, nuts and vanilla extract. Mix well. Pour into prepared pan. Bake 40 to 45 minutes until a toothpick inserted in center comes out clean. Cool 20 minutes in pan. Cut into 2-inch squares. Cool and serve. Makes about 24 bars.

Holiday Fruit Cake

Semisweet chocolate is the secret ingredient.

3/4 cup sifted all-purpose flour
1/2 teaspoon baking powder
1/2 teaspoon salt
1/4 teaspoon baking soda
1 (6-oz.) pkg. semisweet
   chocolate chips (1 cup)
1/2 cup butter or margarine
1/3 cup light-brown sugar, firmly packed

1 teaspoon orange extract
3 eggs
1/2 cup plain yogurt, room temperature
1-3/4 cups finely chopped
   mixed candied fruit
1 cup finely chopped walnuts
Honey-flavored yogurt

Preheat oven to 350°F (175°C). Generously grease and lightly flour a 1-1/2-quart ring mold. Set aside. In a small bowl, mix flour, baking powder, salt and baking soda. Melt chocolate chips in a double boiler. Remove from heat. Set aside to cool. In a large bowl, cream butter or margarine, brown sugar and orange extract until light and fluffy. Add eggs 1 at a time, beating well after each. Stir in melted chocolate. Stir yogurt until creamy. Alternately add flour mixture and yogurt to creamed mixture, beginning and ending with flour mixture. Fold in fruit and walnuts. Pour into prepared ring mold. Bake 25 to 30 minutes. Cool in pan 10 minutes before unmolding. Stir honey-flavored yogurt until creamy. Drizzle over cooled cake. Makes 12 to 14 servings.

Variation

To make miniature fruit cakes, spoon 1/3 cup batter into 12 generously greased 5-ounce custard cups. Bake 20 minutes.

Old-Fashioned Lemon Pound Cake

Something from the good old days.

3-1/2 cups sifted all-purpose flour
1 teaspoon baking soda
1 teaspoon salt
5 eggs, separated
1 cup butter or margarine

2-1/2 cups sugar
1 cup plain yogurt, room temperature
Juice and grated peel of 1 lemon
Sifted powdered sugar, if desired

Preheat oven to 325°F (165°C). Generously grease and lightly flour a 10-inch tube pan. Set aside. Sift together flour, baking soda and salt. In a medium bowl, beat egg whites until stiff. Set aside. Cream butter or margarine in a large bowl. Gradually add sugar. Beat until light and fluffy. In a small bowl, beat egg yolks until thick. Add to creamed mixture. Mix until smooth. Stir yogurt until creamy. Alternately add flour mixture and yogurt to creamed mixture, beginning and ending with flour mixture. Add lemon juice and peel. Gently fold beaten egg whites into batter. Pour into prepared pan. Bake 20 minutes. Increase heat to 350°F (175°C). Bake about 45 to 50 more minutes. Cool in pan on a wire rack. Remove from pan and sprinkle powdered sugar on top of cake, if desired. Makes 1 ring cake.

Blue Ribbon Nut Cake

Celebrate your next important occasion with this superb cake.

Honey Syrup, see below
1 cup sifted all-purpose flour
1-1/2 teaspoons baking powder
1/4 teaspoon salt
1/2 teaspoon cinnamon
3/4 cup butter or margarine
3/4 cup sugar

3 eggs
1/4 cup plain yogurt, room temperature
1/2 teaspoon grated orange peel
1 cup medium chopped walnuts
Whipped cream, for garnish
Maraschino cherries, if desired

Honey Syrup:
1 cup sugar
1/4 cup honey
1/2 cup water

3/4 teaspoon lemon juice
1/2 cup plain yogurt

Prepare Honey Syrup. Set aside to cool. Generously butter an 8-inch square pan. Set aside. Preheat oven to 350°F (175°C). Sift together flour, baking powder, salt and cinnamon. In a large bowl, cream butter or margarine. Gradually add sugar. Beat until light and fluffy. Add eggs 1 at a time, beating well after each. Stir yogurt until creamy. Alternately add flour mixture and yogurt to creamed mixture, beginning and ending with flour mixture. Add orange peel and walnuts. Blend well. Pour into prepared pan. Bake about 30 to 35 minutes. While cake is hot, pour cooled syrup over top. Cool 1 hour before serving. Cut into 2-inch squares. Decorate with whipped cream and maraschino cherry halves, if desired. Makes 16 squares.

Honey Syrup:
In a small saucepan, mix sugar, honey, water and lemon juice. Bring to a boil. Boil gently 7 minutes. Remove from heat. In a small bowl, stir yogurt until creamy. Blend about 2 tablespoons hot syrup into yogurt. Gradually stir yogurt mixture into hot syrup. Boil 2 minutes. Set aside to cool while making cake.

To substitute yogurt for buttermilk in recipes, use water or milk to thin yogurt to the consistency of buttermilk. Generally, replace 1 cup buttermilk with 1/2 to 3/4 cup plain yogurt plus enough water to make 1 cup.

Special Spice Cake

Absolutely perfect with after-dinner coffee or afternoon tea.

2/3 cup shortening
1-1/2 cups sugar
2 eggs
2-1/4 cups sifted cake flour
1-1/2 teaspoons baking soda
1/2 teaspoon salt

1/2 teaspoon nutmeg
1 teaspoon cloves
2 teaspoons cinnamon
1 cup plain yogurt, room temperature
Foamy Frosting, see below

Foamy Frosting:
1 cup sieved light-brown sugar, firmly packed
3 tablespoons cold water

2 egg whites
Few drops vanilla extract

Preheat oven to 350°F (175°C). Generously grease and lightly flour two 8-inch, round cake pans. Set aside. Cream shortening. Add sugar and beat until light and fluffy. Add eggs 1 at a time, beating well after each. Sift together cake flour, baking soda, salt, nutmeg, cloves and cinnamon. Stir yogurt until creamy. Alternately add flour mixture and yogurt to creamed mixture, beginning and ending with flour mixture. Pour into prepared pans. Bake 25 to 30 minutes. Prepare Foamy Frosting. When cool, frost with Foamy Frosting, between layers and on top. Makes one 2-layer cake.

Foamy Frosting:
Place brown sugar, cold water and egg whites in top of a double boiler. Stir well and place over boiling water. Be sure the water in the lower part of double boiler does not touch the upper pan. With a rotary beater, beat constantly 4 to 5 minutes until frosting holds a point. Remove upper pan from boiling water. Add vanilla extract and beat 1 more minute.

Popular Poppy Cookies

Delicate soft cookies to add to your collection.

3 cups all-purpose flour
1 teaspoon salt
1 teaspoon baking soda
1/2 cup butter or margarine
1/2 cup shortening
1 cup sugar

1 egg
1 cup plain yogurt, room temperature
1 teaspoon vanilla extract
1/4 cup poppy seeds
About 1 tablespoon sugar

Preheat oven to 350°F (175°C). Generously grease 2 baking sheets. Set aside. Sift together flour, salt and baking soda. In a large bowl, cream butter or margarine and shortening. Add 1 cup sugar and beat until light and fluffy. Add egg. Beat well. Stir yogurt until creamy. Alternately add flour mixture and yogurt to creamed mixture, beginning and ending with flour mixture. Stir in vanilla extract and poppy seeds. Refrigerate about 3 hours. Drop by teaspoonfuls onto prepared baking sheets. Sprinkle with about 1 tablespoon sugar. Bake 10 to 12 minutes until lightly browned. Makes about 48 cookies.

Glowing Carrot Cake

The smaller and finer the carrot shreds are, the better the cake's texture.

2-1/2 cups sifted cake flour
2 teaspoons baking soda
1 teaspoon cinnamon
3/4 teaspoon ground cloves
1/2 teaspoon mace
1/4 teaspoon allspice
1/4 teaspoon salt
2/3 cup shortening
1 cup sugar

2 eggs
1 cup plus 2 tablespoons plain yogurt,
 room temperature
1/2 cup raisins
1/2 cup currants
1-1/2 cups loosely packed, finely shredded
 carrots (6 medium carrots)
Orange Icing, see below

Orange Icing:
3 tablespoons butter, softened
1-1/2 cups powdered sugar, sifted

1 tablespoon plain yogurt
1 teaspoon grated orange peel

Preheat oven to 350°F (175°C). Generously grease and lightly flour a 9-inch square pan. Set aside. Sift together cake flour, baking soda, cinnamon, cloves, mace, allspice and salt. Cream shortening in a large bowl. Gradually add sugar. Beat until light and fluffy. Add eggs 1 at a time, beating well after each. Stir yogurt until creamy. Alternately add flour mixture and yogurt to creamed mixture, beginning and ending with flour mixture. Fold in raisins, currants and shredded carrots. Pour into prepared pan. Bake 40 to 50 minutes. When cool, frost with Orange Icing. Makes one 9-inch cake.

Orange Icing:
Cream butter. Alternately stir in sugar and yogurt. Add orange peel. Beat until light and fluffy.

Peanut Butter Cookies Supreme

Super good!

1 cup shortening
3/4 cup peanut butter
1 cup light-brown sugar, firmly packed
1/2 cup granulated sugar
1 teaspoon vanilla extract
1 egg, slightly beaten

1/2 cup plain yogurt, room temperature
3 cups all-purpose flour
1 teaspoon baking soda
1/2 teaspoon salt
1 tablespoon all-purpose flour
1 tablespoon granulated sugar

Preheat oven to 375°F (190°C). Cream shortening in a large bowl. Add peanut butter and beat until light and fluffy. Add brown sugar, 1/2 cup granulated sugar and vanilla extract. Beat until light and fluffy. Add egg. Beat well. Stir yogurt until creamy. Blend into creamed mixture. Add 3 cups flour, baking soda and salt. Mix well. Drop by tablespoonfuls 2 inches apart on ungreased baking sheets. In a small cup, mix 1 tablespoon flour and 1 tablespoon sugar. Dip fork into flour-sugar mixture. Press fork criss-cross-fashion on cookies to flatten. Bake 8 to 10 minutes until golden brown. Makes about 48 cookies.

Old World Cookies

One of my family's favorites.

1 cup butter or margarine	6 to 6-3/4 cups all-purpose flour
1-1/2 cups sugar	3 teaspoons baking powder
4 eggs	1 teaspoon baking soda
2 teaspoons vanilla extract	1 egg
1/2 cup plain yogurt, room temperature	1 teaspoon milk

Preheat oven to 350°F (175°C). Generously grease 2 large baking sheets. In a large bowl, cream butter or margarine and sugar until light and fluffy. Beat in 4 eggs and vanilla extract. Mix well. Stir yogurt until creamy. Blend yogurt into creamed mixture. Stir in flour, baking powder and baking soda. Mix well to make a firm dough, adding a little more flour if necessary. Divide dough into 3 equal sections. Shape each section into a long roll about 2 inches in diameter. With a table knife, cut roll into 1/2-inch slices. To make twists, roll each 1/2-inch piece into a 6-inch-long roll. Lift roll, hold in center and twist both sides together to make a 3-inch-long rope. Or shape into braids, snails or other shapes. Place on prepared baking sheets. Repeat with 2 other sections of dough. Beat remaining egg with milk. Brush on cookies. Bake 12 to 15 minutes until lightly browned. Makes about 108 cookies.

Celebration Brownies

Frosted or not, these are the best brownies ever!

3 (1-oz.) squares unsweetened chocolate	1-1/4 cups sugar
1 cup all-purpose flour	3 eggs
1/2 teaspoon baking powder	1 cup plain yogurt, room temperature
1/2 teaspoon salt	1 cup chopped walnuts
1/4 teaspoon baking soda	1-1/4 teaspoons vanilla extract
1/2 cup plus 2 tablespoons butter or margarine	Quick Chocolate Frosting, page 128, if desired

Preheat oven to 350°F (175°C). Generously grease and lightly flour a 9-inch square pan. Set aside. In a double boiler, melt chocolate; set aside to cool. Sift together flour, baking powder, salt and baking soda. Cream butter or margarine in a large bowl. Gradually add sugar, beating until light and fluffy. Add eggs 1 at a time. Stir yogurt until creamy. Alternately add flour mixture and yogurt to creamed mixture, beginning and ending with flour mixture. Stir in cooled chocolate, walnuts and vanilla extract. Bake 50 minutes until a toothpick inserted in center comes out clean. Cool in pan. If desired, frost with Quick Chocolate Frosting. Cut into 2-inch squares. Makes about 16 brownies.

Snow-Cap Sandwiches

These won't stay in the cookie jar for long!

3 cups all-purpose flour
3 teaspoons baking soda
1/2 teaspoon salt
1/2 cup butter or margarine
1-1/2 cups sugar

2 eggs
1 cup plain yogurt, room temperature
2 teaspoons vanilla extract
About 1/2 cup peach or apricot preserves
Powdered sugar

In a medium bowl, sift together flour, baking soda and salt. Cream butter or margarine in a large bowl. Add sugar and beat until light and fluffy. Add eggs 1 at a time, beating after each. Stir yogurt until creamy. Add yogurt and vanilla extract to creamed mixture. Fold flour mixture into yogurt mixture. Mix well. Cover and refrigerate 8 to 10 hours. Preheat oven to 375°F (190°C). Generously grease 2 baking sheets. Drop cookies by teaspoonfuls about 1 inch apart on prepared baking sheets. Bake 8 to 10 minutes until lightly browned. Cool on wire racks. When cooled, place about 1/2 teaspoon preserves on bottom of each cookie. Top with another cookie, making a sandwich. Repeat with remaining cookies. Sprinkle powdered sugar over tops of cookies. Makes about 36 sandwich cookies.

How To Make Snow-Cap Sandwiches

1/Drop dough by teaspoonfuls 1 inch apart on greased baking sheets.

2/Spread 1/2 teaspoon preserves on bottom of one cookie. Place another cookie on top to make a sandwich. Sprinkle tops with powdered sugar.

Sugar Monster Cookies

To delight the children in your life.

1/2 cup shortening	1-1/2 teaspoons baking powder
1 cup sugar	1 teaspoon baking soda
1/2 cup plain yogurt, room temperature	1/2 teaspoon salt
1 egg	1 teaspoon vanilla extract
2-3/4 cups all-purpose flour	About 1 tablespoon sugar

Preheat oven to 350°F (175°C). Generously grease 2 large baking sheets. Set aside. Cream shortening in a large bowl. Add 1 cup sugar and beat until fluffy. Add egg. Mix well. Stir yogurt until creamy. Blend yogurt into creamed mixture. Stir in flour, baking powder, baking soda, salt and vanilla extract. Drop by tablespoonfuls onto prepared baking sheets. Dip the bottom of a custard cup in 1 tablespoon sugar; press cookies to flatten. Dip custard cup in sugar for each cookie. Bake 10 to 12 minutes until lightly browned. Cool on wire racks. Makes about 24 large cookies.

Variation

To make smaller cookies, drop by teaspoonfuls and bake 8 to 10 minutes until lightly browned. Makes about 36 cookies.

Oatmeal-Raisin Cookies

Good to eat and good for you!

1 cup shortening	4 cups quick-cooking oats
1 cup light-brown sugar, firmly packed	1 teaspoon baking powder
1/2 cup granulated sugar	1/2 teaspoon baking soda
1 egg	1 teaspoon cinnamon
1/2 cup plain yogurt, room temperature	1/2 teaspoon salt
1 teaspoon vanilla extract	1 cup raisins

Preheat oven to 350°F (175°C). Lightly grease 2 baking sheets. Set aside. In a large bowl, cream shortening with brown sugar and granulated sugar. Beat until light and fluffy. Stir yogurt until creamy. Blend egg, yogurt and vanilla extract into creamed mixture. Stir in oats, baking powder, baking soda, cinnamon, salt and raisins. Drop by tablespoonfuls 2 inches apart on prepared baking sheets. Bake about 15 minutes until golden brown. Cool slightly. Remove from baking sheets. Makes about 60 cookies.

Elegant Desserts

Dessert lovers will be enchanted with yogurt. The desserts in this section are easy to make and deliciously different, and many are low in calories.

Keep some pound cake in the freezer for unexpected company. You can quickly put together Apricot Delight or Coconut Luau Strips. Mocha Torte satisfies the coffee taste many people enjoy after a meal. It's glamorous, but easy to make.

For a quick dessert, blend fruit-flavored yogurt with instant vanilla pudding. Layer it with fruit in graceful parfait glasses.

I don't have to tell you how much I enjoyed creating and tasting these desserts. I gained about— but let's not talk about that. It was fun!

1/Line a 7-inch bowl with foil, allowing several inches to extend over the edge. Press softened Raspberry Frozen Yogurt into bottom of bowl. Level the top.

2/To make a layered effect, place Crème de Menthe Frozen Yogurt over the Raspberry Frozen Yogurt. Level the top and add Chocolate Frozen Yogurt. Cover and freeze overnight.

How To Make Baked Alaska Flambé

3/Place a white cake on a water-soaked wooden board. Carefully unmold frozen yogurt on center of cake. Peel off foil.

4/Completely cover cake and frozen yogurt with meringue, sealing well to the board. Make sure there are no air pockets or holes between the meringue, the frozen yogurt and the cake. With cake still on board, brown meringue. The completed Baked Alaska Flambé appears on the front cover of this book.

Baked Alaska Flambé

Yogurt salutes Alaska.

3 cups Raspberry Frozen Yogurt, page 152
3 cups Crème de Menthe Frozen Yogurt,
   page 157
2 cups Chocolate Frozen Yogurt, page 154
3/4 cup sugar

1-1/4 cups egg whites (about 10)
1/2 teaspoon cream of tartar
1 (9-inch) white cake
2 tablespoons brandy

Line a 7-inch bowl with aluminum foil, allowing 3 to 5 inches of foil to extend over edge. Slightly soften the frozen yogurts. Press Raspberry Frozen Yogurt into bottom of foil-lined bowl; level the top. Add Crème de Menthe Frozen Yogurt. Cover with Chocolate Frozen Yogurt. Do not mix layers. Cover and freeze 8 to 10 hours. Soak a wooden board in water about 2 hours to prevent scorching; dry with a towel. Put sugar and egg whites in a large bowl. Let stand 30 minutes. Preheat oven to 450°F (230°C.) Beat egg white mixture until frothy. Add cream of tartar. Beat until stiff peaks are formed. Place white cake on wooden board. Unmold frozen yogurt onto center of cake. Peel off aluminum foil. Cover completely with meringue, sealing cake to board. Be sure there are no air pockets between meringue and frozen yogurts. Lightly brown on board in preheated oven 3 to 5 minutes. If desired, place cake, still on board, on a 14-inch, round serving tray. To flame, place brandy in a small saucepan and heat. Do not boil. Ignite brandy with a long match. Pour flaming brandy over Baked Alaska. Use a serrated knife dipped in water to cut cake. Makes about 14 servings.

Custard Torte

Bravissimo!

1/2 cup sugar
5 eggs
1 cup sugar
1/4 teaspoon salt

1 teaspoon vanilla extract
3 cups plain yogurt
1 tablespoon cornstarch

Preheat oven to 475°F. (245°C). Put 1/2 cup sugar in a large heavy skillet. With a wooden spoon, stir constantly over low heat until sugar dissolves and turns to a golden syrup. Immediately pour into a 5-cup ring mold. While syrup is still in liquid state, tilt mold to coat the sides. Set aside to cool. Caramelized sugar will harden. In a large bowl, beat eggs, 1 cup sugar, salt and vanilla extract. In a small bowl, stir yogurt and cornstarch until creamy. Blend into egg-sugar mixture, beating until smooth but not frothy. Measure 1 cup mixture; set aside. Pour remaining mixture into caramel-lined mold. Place mold in a deep baking pan in middle of preheated oven. Add remaining mixture. Pour hot water 1 inch deep into baking pan. Bake 5 minutes. Reduce heat to 425°F (220°C). Bake 40 more minutes until a knife inserted near center comes out clean. Do not overbake. Remove mold from hot water. Refrigerate about 24 hours. Custard will settle as it cools. Unmold by running a thin spatula around edge of mold; place serving platter on top of mold and invert. To serve, spoon caramel sauce over each serving. Makes about 8 servings.

Cherry Jubilee

Take out your chafing dish and celebrate!

1 (1-lb. 4-oz.) can pitted dark,
   sweet cherries
4 teaspoons cornstarch
1 cup currant jelly

1 cup cherry-flavored yogurt
1/4 cup brandy
1 pint vanilla ice cream

Drain cherries; reserve juice. In a medium saucepan, mix 1 tablespoon cherry juice and cornstarch. Stir in jelly. Heat over low heat until slightly thickened. In a small bowl, stir yogurt until creamy. Blend about 2 tablespoons hot sauce into yogurt. Gradually add yogurt-sauce mixture to remaining sauce. Simmer gently until thickened. Remove from heat. Fold in drained cherries. Warm brandy in a small saucepan over low heat. Do not boil. With a long match ignite brandy. Pour flaming brandy over sauce. Spoon immediately over ice cream. Makes about 6 servings.

Perfect Peach Fluff

A heavenly finish to a hearty meal.

1 (6-oz.) pkg. peach-flavored gelatin
1-1/2 cups boiling water

2 cups plain yogurt
1 (8-oz.) can sliced peaches, drained

Generously oil a 5-cup ring mold; set aside. In a medium bowl, dissolve gelatin in boiling water. Refrigerate 5 minutes. Stir yogurt until creamy. Gradually blend yogurt into gelatin. Fold in peaches. Pour into prepared mold. Refrigerate until firm. Invert to unmold and serve. Makes about 8 servings.

Fruit Pudding

Instant pudding makes a quick and different dessert.

1 (3-3/4-oz.) pkg. instant vanilla pudding mix
2 cups any flavor fruit yogurt

Put pudding mix and yogurt in a small bowl. Beat with an electric mixer on low speed about 2 minutes until smooth and thick. Pour into 4 individual 1/2-cup serving dishes. Makes 4 servings.

Variation
Place pudding-yogurt mixture in parfait glasses and alternate layers of fresh fruit with pudding. Do not use bananas unless dessert is served immediately.

Fresh Fruit Medley

Delightfully refreshing.

1 cup plain yogurt
2 tablespoons brown sugar
2 small peaches, peeled and diced
2 small pears, diced

1 large apple, diced
1/2 cup blueberries
1/2 cup coarsely chopped walnuts

In a small bowl, stir yogurt until creamy. Blend in brown sugar. In a large bowl, gently toss together peaches, pears, apple and blueberries. Pour yogurt mixture over fruit. Toss gently. Sprinkle walnuts over top. Makes about 4 servings.

Banana Pick-Me-Up

A nutritious snack or dessert. Good for breakfast, too.

1 small banana
1/4 cup plain yogurt

1/2 teaspoon brown sugar

Slice banana. In a small bowl, blend yogurt with brown sugar. Spoon over banana and serve immediately. Makes 1 serving.

Variation
Substitute pears, peaches, cantaloupe or berries for the banana.

Chocolate Yogurt Fondue

Have fun with this one.

4 (1-oz.) squares semisweet chocolate
3/4 cup sugar
1/2 cup Half-and-Half Yogurt, page 15,
   room temperature

3 tablespoons kirsch liqueur
Pieces of fruit or cake for dipping

Put chocolate and sugar in a 2-cup fondue pot. Heat and stir until chocolate melts and mixture is smooth. Stir yogurt until creamy. Gradually add to chocolate mixture. Blend in kirsch liqueur. Keep fondue warm over low heat. If you do not have a fondue pot, heat mixture in top of a double boiler and keep fondue warm over hot water. With fondue forks, twirl pieces of fruit or cake in fondue. Makes about 1-1/2 cups.

Mocha Torte

Divinely different.

1 (11-1/2-oz.) rectangular angel food cake
24 large marshmallows
1 (6-oz.) pkg. semisweet chocolate chips (1 cup)

1 teaspoon instant coffee powder
1/2 cup coffee-flavored yogurt

Cut cake crosswise into 5 horizontal layers. Set aside. In a double boiler or heavy sauce pan with non-stick surface, melt marshmallows, chocolate chips, coffee powder and coffee yogurt over low heat, stirring. Refrigerate icing until partially set. Spread a thin layer of icing over each cake layer. Stack layers. Cover entire cake with remaining icing. Makes about 8 servings.

Coconut Luau Strips

Yogurt goes Hawaiian!

1 (10-3/4-oz.) pkg. frozen pound cake
3/4 cup plain yogurt

1/3 cup honey
1 (7-oz.) pkg. shredded coconut

With a knife, trim crusts from cake. Cut cake crosswise into 1/2-inch-thick slices. Cut each slice in half lengthwise to form strips. In a small bowl, beat yogurt and honey together until creamy. Dip cake strips into yogurt-honey mixture. Roll in shredded coconut. Place on baking sheet. Broil about 4 inches from heat, 5 to 6 minutes until lightly browned. Turn carefully. Broil 3 to 5 minutes on other side. Cool. Makes about 16 strips.

Apricot Delight

Easy to make and a joy to eat.

4 slices pound cake, 1/2-inch thick
12 apricot halves, fresh or canned
2 cups plain yogurt or Whipping Cream
   Yogurt, page 15

Whipped cream, for garnish
4 maraschino cherries, for garnish

Place cake slices in 4 individual serving dishes. Arrange apricot halves on top of cake slices. Stir yogurt until creamy. Pour 1/2 cup yogurt over each slice. If desired, top each with whipped cream and a maraschino cherry. Makes 4 servings.

Quick Boston Cream Pie

Make a luscious dessert with package mixes.

2 (9-inch) baked yellow cake layers
1 cup milk
1/2 cup plain yogurt
1 (3-3/4-oz.) pkg. instant vanilla pudding
   and pie filling mix

1 (6-oz.) pkg. semisweet chocolate chips (1 cup)
1/4 cup plain yogurt

Place 1 cake layer on a large cake platter. Set aside. Pour milk and 1/2 cup yogurt into a small bowl. Add pudding mix. Beat with electric mixer on low speed about 2 minutes until well-blended. Spread filling evenly over cake. Top with second cake layer. Melt chocolate chips in a double boiler over boiling water. Remove from heat. Stir 1/4 cup yogurt until creamy. Gradually stir into melted chocolate. Spread evenly over top of cake, letting frosting drizzle over side. Makes about 10 servings.

Frosty Lemon Fluff

Invite the neighbors over for a treat.

3/4 cup sugar
3 eggs
1/2 cup water
1 (4-1/2-oz.) pkg. lemon pudding and
   pie-filling mix

2 cups plain yogurt
1 (15-oz.) can sweetened condensed milk
4 teaspoons lemon juice
Grated peel of 1 lemon

Combine sugar and eggs in a medium saucepan. Beat well. Stir in water. Add pudding mix. Blend well. Cook and stir over medium heat until thickened and bubbly. Remove from heat. Cool slightly. In a large bowl, stir yogurt until creamy. Gradually beat in sweetened condensed milk, lemon juice and grated lemon peel. Stir cooled lemon pudding mixture into yogurt mixture. Pour into a 13" x 9" glass baking dish. Freeze 3 to 4 hours. Remove from freezer and let stand at room temperature 15 to 20 minutes before serving. Cut into 2" x 3" pieces. Makes about 18 pieces.

For a quick dessert, top banana slices with strawberry-flavored yogurt; sprinkle with chopped nuts or flaked coconut.

Strawberry Party Tarts

Fresh berries covered with a smooth glaze and whipped cream.

4 cups fresh strawberries
1/2 cup water
1 cup sugar
2 tablespoons cornstarch
1/2 cup plain yogurt, room temperature

Few drops red food coloring
8 (3-inch) baked pastry tart shells or
   graham cracker tart shells
Whipped cream, for garnish

Wash and hull strawberries. In a 1-quart saucepan, crush 1 cup of the smaller berries and cook in 1/2 cup water about 3 minutes. Press cooked berries through a sieve. Return to saucepan. Stir sugar and cornstarch together. Add to berry juice. Cook and stir until clear and thickened. In a small bowl, stir yogurt until creamy. Blend about 2 tablespoons of hot thickened glaze into yogurt. Carefully stir yogurt mixture into remaining glaze. Cook and stir 3 to 5 minutes. Remove from heat. Stir in food coloring. Set aside to cool. Slice remaining strawberries into tart shells. Pour cooled glaze evenly over berries. Refrigerate 4 hours before serving. Decorate with whipped cream. Makes about 8 servings.

Variation
Substitute 3 cups fresh raspberries for strawberries; do not slice before putting into tart shells.

Pumpkin Chiffon Pie

Elegant, yet so easy to make.

1 tablespoon unflavored gelatin
1/4 cup cold water
3 eggs, separated
1 (16-oz.) can solid-pack pumpkin
1/2 cup granulated sugar
1/2 cup light brown sugar,
  firmly packed
1 teaspoon cinnamon

1/2 teaspoon salt
1/8 teaspoon ginger
1/8 teaspoon ground cloves
1 teaspoon cornstarch
1/2 cup plain yogurt, room temperature
6 tablespoons granulated sugar
1 (9-inch) pie shell, baked and cooled

Soak gelatin in cold water to soften. In a small bowl, beat egg yolks until thickened. Mash pumpkin in a medium saucepan. Add beaten yolks, 1/2 cup granulated sugar, brown sugar, cinnamon, salt, ginger, cloves and cornstarch. Cook and stir over low heat about 5 minutes until thickened. Add softened gelatin mixture and stir to dissolve. Remove from heat. In a small bowl, stir yogurt until creamy. Blend about 2 tablespoons pumpkin mixture into yogurt. Gradually add yogurt-pumpkin mixture to remaining pumpkin mixture. Mix well. Refrigerate until mixture thickens. Beat egg whites until stiff. Gradually add 6 tablespoons sugar, 1 tablespoon at a time. Gently fold beaten egg white mixture into pumpkin mixture. Pour into baked and cooled pie shell. Refrigerate 4 to 5 hours. Makes about 8 servings.

Individual Lemon Meringues

Each one will have a look of its own!

3/4 cup egg whites, room temperature
1-1/2 teaspoons cream of tartar
1/4 teaspoon salt

1-1/2 cups super-fine sugar
1 teaspoon vanilla extract
Lemon-Yogurt Filling, see below

Lemon-Yogurt Filling:
3 cups plain yogurt

2 (3-3/4-oz.) pkgs. instant lemon pudding
  and pie-filling mix

Preheat oven to 275°F (135°C). Line a baking sheet with brown paper. Put egg whites, cream of tartar and salt in a large bowl. Beat until foamy. Add sugar gradually, beating until meringue is stiff and holds its shape. Beat in vanilla extract. With a rubber scraper and a spoon, shape meringue into eight 3-inch rings with sides about 1-1/2 inches high, on prepared baking sheet. Bake 45 to 50 minutes until lightly browned. Prepare Lemon-Yogurt Filling while meringues are baking. Cool meringues on baking sheet 5 minutes. Remove from paper. Cool thoroughly on a wire rack. Fill each meringue ring with Lemon-Yogurt Filling. Makes 8 meringues.

Lemon-Yogurt Filling:
Put yogurt and lemon pudding mix in a large bowl. Beat with electric mixer on low speed about 2 minutes until well-blended. Refrigerate 30 minutes.

Lemon Meringue Pie

Disappears as soon as you put it on the table.

1 (3-oz.) pkg. lemon pudding and
  pie-filling mix
1/2 cup sugar
1/4 cup water

2 egg yolks
2 cups lemon-flavored yogurt
1 (8-inch) baked pie shell
Fluffy Meringue, see below

Fluffy Meringue:
2 egg whites
1/8 teaspoon cream of tartar

2 tablespoons sugar

In a medium saucepan, combine lemon pudding mix, sugar and water. Beat egg yolks slightly. Stir yolks into pudding mixture. Cook and stir over low heat about 2 minutes. Remove from heat. Stir yogurt until creamy. Blend into pudding mixture. Cook and stir until thickened. Remove from heat. Cool 5 minutes; stir twice while cooling. Pour into pie shell. Refrigerate 4 hours. Prepare Fluffy Meringue. Cover chilled pie with meringue, sealing well. Preheat oven to 425°F (220°C). Bake about 5 minutes. Serve immediately. Makes about 6 servings.

Fluffy Meringue:
Beat egg whites until foamy. Add cream of tartar. Add sugar 1 tablespoon at a time. Beat until stiff.

Individual Lemon Meringues

Traditional Apple Pie

Improved with yogurt!

6 cups peeled and sliced apples
   (6 to 7 baking apples)
1/2 cup granulated sugar
1 tablespoon all-purpose flour

1 teaspoon cinnamon
1 (9-inch) unbaked pie shell
2 tablespoons butter or margarine
Yogurt Crumb Topping, see below

Yogurt Crumb Topping:
1/2 cup all-purpose flour
1/2 cup light-brown sugar, firmly packed
1/2 teaspoon cinnamon

1/4 cup hard butter or margarine
1/2 cup plain yogurt, room temperature

Preheat oven to 375°F (190°C). In a large bowl, toss apples, granulated sugar, flour and cinnamon. Arrange in unbaked pie shell. Dot with butter or margarine. Bake 45 minutes. Prepare Yogurt Crumb Topping. Remove pie from oven. Spread Yogurt Crumb Topping evenly over apples. Bake 10 to 15 minutes until golden brown. Makes 6 servings.

Yogurt Crumb Topping:
In a small bowl, cut flour, brown sugar and cinnamon into butter or margarine. Stir yogurt into crumb topping. Blend well.

How To Make Traditional Apple Pie

1/Partially bake apple mixture in unbaked pie shell. Blend yogurt into crumb topping mixture.

2/Spread Yogurt Crumb Topping evenly over partially baked apples. Bake until golden brown.

Chocolate Yogurt Pie

Spoil your family and friends with this one.

Coconut Crust, see below
1 (5-1/4-oz.) pkg. chocolate pudding
   and pie-filling mix
1-3/4 cups milk

1 cup plain yogurt, room temperature
1 tablespoon crème de cacao
1/2 teaspoon vanilla extract
Whipped cream, for garnish

Coconut Crust:
2 cups flaked coconut
3 tablespoons butter or margarine, melted

Prepare Coconut Crust. Set aside. In a medium saucepan, stir together pudding mix and milk. Bring to a boil, stirring constantly. Cook and stir 1 minute. Remove from heat. Stir yogurt until creamy. Gradually stir yogurt into chocolate pudding mixture. Add creme de cacao and vanilla extract. Pour into cooled crust. Refrigerate 6 to 7 hours. Serve garnished with whipped cream. Makes about 8 servings.

Coconut Crust:
Preheat oven to 325°F (165°C). Put coconut in a medium bowl. Pour butter or margarine over coconut. Toss to coat evenly. Press onto bottom and sides of a 9-inch pie plate. Bake 15 to 20 minutes until lightly browned. Cool.

Graham Cracker Crust

Try this marvelous crumb crust with your favorite pie filling.

1 cup crushed graham crackers,
   about 12 crackers
2 tablespoons plain yogurt

1/4 teaspoon cinnamon
1 tablespoon sugar

Preheat oven to 350°F (175°C). Combine all ingredients in a small bowl. Press into a 9-inch pie plate or spring-form pan. Bake 7 minutes. Set aside to cool while preparing filling. Makes one 9-inch pie crust.

Variation

To make tart shells, press crust mixture into six 3-inch tart pans.

Frozen Yogurt

Frozen desserts are convenient because they can be prepared in advance. If you have a dinner menu with a lot of preparation, consider serving a frozen yogurt dessert to cut down on the last-minute rush. Your guests are sure to enjoy Fruited Frozen Yogurt or Tutti Frutti Sherbet.

Making your own frozen yogurt is fun. Mix the ingredients, put them in a glass dish to prevent a metallic taste and put in the freezer until semi-frozen. Then the mixture is beaten to give it a creamy texture. You can make frozen yogurt even lighter in texture by repeating the freezing and beating 2 or 3 times. Make sure the partially frozen yogurt still has some ice crystals after beating. Do not overbeat it. If you have an ice cream maker, follow the manufacturer's instructions.

I use both Half-and-Half Yogurt, page 15, and Plain Yogurt, page 13, for the recipes in this section. If you're watching calories, use Plain Yogurt. The results are satisfying and delicious.

Making frozen yogurt is a family project in our house. It's a fun group activity. You can enjoy the fruits of your labors right away or store them in the freezer for up to 10 days.

HAWAIIAN LUAU PARTY
Aloha Fruit & Dip, page 35
Pork Kabobs
Crab Roll-Ups
Hawaiian Chicken
Asparagus Spears
Coconut Luau Strips, page 142
Raspberry Frozen Yogurt, page 152
Tea

CHILDREN'S PARTY
Corn Dogs
Potato Chips
Popcorn
Peanut Butter Cookies Supreme, page 133
Frozen Pops, page 159
Lemonade

NEIGHBORHOOD GET-TOGETHER
Spicy Fruit Punch
Pretzel Sticks
Nuts
Peach Frozen Yogurt, page 155
Butter Cookies
Coffee & Tea

SWEET SIXTEEN
Super Sloppy Joes, page 64
Potato Salad
Crisp Relishes
Peanuts
Sugar Monster Cookies, page 136
Cherry Swirl Ice Cake, page 158
Fruit Drink

Fruited Frozen Yogurt

My favorite frozen yogurt ice cream.

Sweetened Fruit, see below
2-1/4 cups water
3/4 cup sugar
1 cup white corn syrup

1 teaspoon unflavored gelatin
1 quart plain yogurt
2 teaspoons vanilla extract

Sweetened Fruit:
3 cups fresh or frozen strawberries, cherries,
   raspberries or blueberries

2/3 cup sugar

Prepare Sweetened Fruit. In a 3-quart saucepan, mix water, sugar, corn syrup and gelatin. Heat almost to boiling. Remove from heat and cool. Stir yogurt until creamy. Slowly blend into cooled syrup. Pour into a 13" x 9" glass baking dish. Freeze about 1 hour until partially frozen: Spoon into a large chilled bowl. Beat with electric mixer at low speed about 30 seconds until smooth and airy but not completely thawed. Do not overbeat. Mixture will contain some ice crystals. Fold in vanilla extract and Sweetened Fruit. Place in a 2-quart freezer container. Cover and freeze 1 to 2 hours to soft or semifrozen stage. Makes about 2 quarts.

Sweetened Fruit:
Place fruit in a small bowl with lid. Cut strawberries or cherries in half. Leave raspberries or blueberries whole. If using frozen unsweetened fruit, thaw and drain. Sprinkle fruit with sugar. Mix well. Cover and refrigerate 24 to 48 hours.

Variations
Almond Frozen Yogurt: Omit vanilla extract and add 1 teaspoon almond extract. Substitute 1 cup toasted slivered almonds for Sweetened Fruit.
Pecan Frozen Yogurt: Substitute 1 cup chopped pecans and 1 tablespoon molasses for Sweetened Fruit.
Pineapple Frozen Yogurt: Substitute 1 (1-lb. 4-oz.) can drained, sweetened or unsweetened crushed pineapple for 3 cups fresh or frozen fruit. Then mix with sugar. Replace part of the 2-1/4 cups water with drained liquid.

Mocha Topping

A delicious coffee flavor.

1-1/2 teaspoons instant coffee
1/2 teaspoon hot water

1/2 cup coffee-flavored yogurt
2 cups sifted powdered sugar

Dissolve coffee in hot water. In a small bowl, blend yogurt until creamy. Stir in powdered sugar and dissolved coffee. Blend well. Serve over ice cream. Makes about 1 cup.

Raspberry Frozen Yogurt

You'll enjoy the tantalizing taste.

1 (3-oz.) pkg. raspberry-flavored gelatin
1 cup boiling water
1 cup sugar

2 eggs
2 cups Half-and-Half Yogurt, page 15,
   or plain yogurt

Put gelatin in a medium bowl. Pour boiling water over gelatin and stir to dissolve. Add sugar and stir to dissolve. Cool slightly. In a medium bowl, beat eggs with electric mixer on medium speed until thickened. Reduce speed to low. Gradually beat in yogurt and slightly cooled gelatin mixture. Pour into an 11" x 7" glass baking dish. Freeze 1 hour until mixture is partially frozen. Spoon into a large chilled bowl. Beat with electric mixer on low speed about 30 seconds until smooth and airy but not completely thawed. Do not overbeat. Mixture will contain some ice crystals. Place in a 1-quart freezer container. Cover and freeze 1 to 2 hours to soft of semifrozen stage. Makes about 1 quart.

Fruit Cocktail Squares

A new fruit cocktail fashion!

1 cup Half-and-Half Yogurt, page 15
   or plain yogurt
1 (14-oz.) can sweetened condensed milk

1 cup marshmallow creme
1 (17-oz.) can fruit cocktail, well-drained
1 (1-lb. 5-oz.) can peach pie filling

In a large bowl, beat yogurt with electric mixer on low speed until light and airy. Gradually add sweetened condensed milk and marshmallow creme, blending well. Fold in fruit cocktail and pie filling. Pour into an 11" x 7" glass baking dish. Freeze about 4 hours until partially frozen. If completely frozen, let stand at room temperature about 10 minutes before serving. Pie should be semifrozen for serving. Cut into 2-inch squares. Makes about 15 servings.

Peach Melbas

A spin-off from the classic elegant dessert.

2 (10-oz.) pkgs. frozen raspberries
2 tablespoons cornstarch
1/2 teaspoon rum flavoring
1 teaspoon lemon juice

8 scoops Peach Frozen Yogurt, page 155
8 small sponge cakes, about 4 inches
   in diameter

Drain raspberries; reserve juice. In a small saucepan, mix cornstarch with raspberry juice. Cook and stir until thickened. Reduce heat and cook 5 minutes. Stir in rum flavoring, lemon juice and raspberries. Heat to serving temperature. Place a scoop of Peach Frozen Yogurt on each cake. Pour warm sauce over each serving. Makes 8 servings.

Chocolate Frozen Yogurt

So velvety rich and creamy.

1 cup marshmallow creme
1 cup chocolate-flavored syrup
2 cups Half-and-Half Yogurt, page 15
   or plain yogurt
2 eggs

In a large bowl, beat marshmallow creme and chocolate syrup until creamy, scraping sides frequently. Gradually add yogurt, beating well. In a small bowl, beat eggs until thickened. Gradually add eggs to yogurt-chocolate mixture, beating well. Pour into an 11" x 7" glass baking dish. Freeze 1 hour until mixture is partially frozen. Spoon into a large chilled bowl. Beat with electric mixer on low speed about 30 seconds until smooth and airy but not completely thawed. Do not overbeat. Mixture will contain some ice crystals. Place in a 1-quart freezer container. Cover and freeze 1 to 2 hours to soft or semifrozen stage. Makes about 3 cups.

Variation
To make Fudge Pops, put Chocolate Frozen Yogurt into paper cups. Freeze about 30 minutes until partially firm. Place a wooden stick in center of each cup and freeze until hard.

Tutti Frutti Sherbet

Do yourself a favor! Try this refreshing fruit blend.

3/4 cup orange juice
1 cup plain or fruit-flavored yogurt
1/2 cup honey

1 cup fresh or frozen strawberries
   or raspberries
1/2 cup drained crushed pineapple

Put orange juice, yogurt, honey, strawberries or raspberries and pineapple in a blender. Cover and blend on medium speed until smooth. Pour into an 11" x 7" glass baking dish. Freeze 1 hour until mixture is partially frozen. Spoon into a large chilled bowl. Beat with electric mixer on low speed about 30 seconds until smooth and airy but not completely thawed. Do not overbeat. Mixture will contain some ice crystals. Place in a 1-quart freezer container. Cover and freeze 1 to 2 hours to soft or semifrozen stage. Makes about 1 quart.

Frozen yogurt is best when served partially frozen. If it's frozen hard, let soften in refrigerator about 30 minutes before serving.

Peach Frozen Yogurt

A real peachy taste!

1 envelope unflavored gelatin	1/2 cup sugar
1/4 cup cold water	4 cups Half-and-Half Yogurt, page 15
2 cups fresh or frozen sliced peaches	or plain yogurt

In a small saucepan, sprinkle gelatin over cold water. Stir over low heat to dissolve. Put sliced peaches, sugar and yogurt in a blender. Cover and blend on high speed until smooth. Add dissolved gelatin. Cover and blend again. Pour into a 13" x 9" glass baking dish. Freeze 1 hour until mixture is partially frozen. Spoon into a large chilled bowl. Beat with electric mixer on low speed about 30 seconds until smooth and airy but not completely thawed. Do not overbeat. Mixture will contain some ice crystals. Place in a 1-1/2-quart freezer container. Cover and freeze 1 to 2 hours to soft or semifrozen stage. Makes about 1-1/2 quarts.

No-Crust Apple Pie

This is the apple pie to serve on a warm summer evening.

1-1/2 cups plain yogurt	1/4 cup chopped walnuts
1 tablespoon brown sugar	1 (1-lb. 5-oz.) can apple pie filling
1/3 cup raisins	

In a large bowl, beat yogurt and brown sugar until light and airy. By hand, fold in raisins, walnuts and apple pie filling. Pour into a 9-inch glass pie plate. Freeze 4 hours until partially frozen. Serve partially frozen. If pie is completely frozen, let stand at room temperature about 10 minutes before serving. Makes about 8 servings.

Nutty Chocolate Sauce

Especially good over vanilla ice cream.

1/4 cup butter or margarine	1/2 cup vanilla-flavored yogurt,
1 cup coarsely chopped peanuts	room temperature
1 (6-oz.) pkg. semisweet chocolate chips	
(1 cup)	

Melt butter or margarine in a large heavy skillet with nonstick surface or in a double boiler. Add peanuts. Sauté and stir until golden brown. Remove from heat. Add chocolate chips. Stir until chocolate melts and mixture is blended. Stir yogurt until creamy. Fold into chocolate mixture. Serve warm over ice cream. Makes about 1-1/2 cups.

1/Dissolve lime gelatin and sugar in a medium bowl. In a large bowl, beat eggs until thick. Gradually stir in yogurt.

How To Make Crème de Menthe Frozen Yogurt

2/Freeze 1 hour until partially frozen. The middle will be semifrozen or slushy.

3/Chill a large bowl and beaters. Beat semifrozen yogurt mixture on low speed until smooth and airy but not completely thawed. Store in plastic containers in freezer.

Crème de Menthe Frozen Yogurt

A delight in every bite.

1 (3-oz.) pkg. lime-flavored gelatin
1 cup boiling water
1 cup sugar
2 eggs

2 cups Half-and-Half Yogurt, page 15
   or plain yogurt
1/4 cup crème de menthe liqueur

Put gelatin in a medium bowl. Pour boiling water over gelatin and stir to dissolve. Add sugar and stir to dissolve. Cool slightly. In a large bowl, beat eggs until thickened. Gradually add yogurt, beating well. Beat in slightly cooled gelatin mixture and crème de menthe liqueur. Pour into an 11" x 7" glass baking dish. Freeze 1 hour until mixture is partially frozen. Spoon into a large chilled bowl. Beat with electric mixer on low speed 30 seconds until smooth and airy but not completely thawed. Do not overbeat. Mixture will contain some ice crystals. Place in a 1-quart freezer container. Cover and freeze 1 to 2 hours to soft or semifrozen stage. Makes about 1 quart.

Apple Praline Parfait

They'll ask for your recipe.

1 (1-lb. 4-oz.) can sliced apples
1/2 cup granulated sugar
2 cups Half-and-Half Yogurt, page 15
   or plain yogurt
1 (7-oz.) jar marshmallow creme
1/4 cup apricot brandy
1 (4-1/2-oz.) carton nondairy
   whipped topping

1/2 cup light-brown sugar, firmly packed
1/2 cup chopped pecans
1 tablespoon molasses
Whipped cream, for garnish
Maraschino cherries, for garnish

Drain apples, cut into cubes and put in a colander. Place colander in a large bowl. Sprinkle with 1/2 cup granulated sugar. Refrigerate 8 to 10 hours. In a large bowl, beat yogurt until light and airy. Beat in marshmallow creme and apricot brandy. By hand, fold in apple cubes and nondairy whipped topping. Pour into an 11" x 7" glass baking dish. In a small bowl, mix brown sugar, pecans and molasses. Place on top of yogurt mixture. With a knife, cut zig zags through yogurt mixture to give a swirled effect. Freeze 2 hours. Spoon into parfait glasses. Garnish with whipped cream and maraschino cherries. Makes 8 to 10 parfaits.

Blueberry Marshmallow Creme

The more you eat, the more you want.

1/2 lb. fresh or frozen unsweetened
  blueberries, thawed and drained (2 cups)
1/4 cup sugar
1 cup Half-and-Half Yogurt, page 15
  or plain yogurt

1 (14-oz.) can sweetened condensed milk
1 (1-lb. 5-oz.) can blueberry pie filling
1 (4-1/2-oz.) carton nondairy
  whipped topping
1/2 cup marshmallow topping

In a small bowl, sprinkle blueberries with sugar. Cover and let stand 8 to 10 hours. Drain. In a large bowl, beat yogurt until light and airy. Gradually add sweetened condensed milk, beating well. Fold in pie filling, whipped topping and drained blueberries. Pour into an 11" x 7" glass baking dish. Swirl in marshmallow topping, giving marbled effect. Freeze about 4 hours until partially frozen. If completely frozen, let stand at room temperature about 15 minutes before serving. Cut into 2-inch squares. Makes about 15 servings.

Variation
Serve in parfait glasses, alternating layers of Blueberry Marshmallow Creme with fresh blueberries. Top with whipped cream.

Cherry Swirl Ice Cake

You can decorate it like a birthday cake with candles and trimmings.

2 cups Half-and-Half Yogurt, page 15
  or plain yogurt

1 (14-oz.) can sweetened condensed milk
1 (1-lb. 5-oz.) can cherry pie filling

Cover bottom of a 9-inch, round cake pan with wax paper. In a large bowl, beat yogurt until light and airy. Gradually add sweetened condensed milk, beating well. Fold in cherry pie filling, making a swirled effect. Pour into prepared cake pan. Freeze about 4 hours until partially frozen. Invert to unmold. If cake is completely frozen, let stand at room temperature about 10 minutes before serving. Makes 8 to 10 servings.

Variation
Substitute blueberry, strawberry or peach pie filling for the cherry pie filling.

Make shakes with delicious flavors by using frozen yogurt instead of ice cream.

Frozen Pops

Kids love 'em!

2 cups strawberry-flavored or plain yogurt
2 cups fresh or thawed frozen strawberries

2 tablespoons strawberry preserves

Put yogurt, strawberries and preserves in a blender. Cover and blend on high speed about 1 minute to puree strawberries. Pour into six 4-ounce paper cups. Freeze about 30 minutes until partially firm. Stand a wooden stick in center of each cup. Freeze until pops are hard. Peel off paper cup and serve. Makes 6 pops.

Variation

Substitute blueberry or raspberry-flavored yogurt, fresh or thawed frozen blueberries or raspberries, and blueberry or raspberry preserves for strawberry ingredients.

How To Make Frozen Pops

1/Freeze pops in paper cups until partially firm. Place a wooden stick in center of each cup.

2/Peel off paper cups before serving.

Yogo-Cheese

It's unique! You can't buy it in a store—you make it yourself! And no matter how often you make it, you won't be able to keep up with the demand. I'm talking about Yogo-Cheese. Creamy and white, Yogo-Cheese tastes like American cream cheese or French Neufchatel, but it has fewer calories.

Yogo-Cheese is easy to make, but be sure to use your own homemade yogurt. For the best results use the recipes for Plain Yogurt, page 13, or Whole Milk Yogurt, page 14. Then turn to the Yogo-Cheese recipe, page 161.

You can use Yogo-Cheese in appetizers, main dishes and soufflés. Try Grand Mariner Soufflé for an elegant supper. Friends coming for dinner? Impress them with Stuffed Meat Rolls and Swirled Strawberry Pie. Something to go with afternoon coffee? How about the Tasty Cheese Cubes you made the night before? Served plain or with a few herbs or spices mixed in, Yogo-Cheese is delicious as a spread for crackers, toast or as a sandwich spread.

You'll add this new wholesome gourmet food to your table with the same satisfaction you get from serving your own baked bread or tossing a salad with vegetables from your own garden.

SUPER SUPPER
Surprise Pork Chops, page 166
Chunky Applesauce
Herb-Stuffed Baked Potatoes, page 100
Vegetable Medley
Cherry Pie a la Mode
Tea

SPRING SHOWER
Crabmeat Soufflé
Strawberry Surprise Mold, page 170
Fancy Dinner Rolls, page 122
Miniature Cream Puffs
Lemonade

COFFEE KLATCH
Easy Danish Pastry, page 163
Cherry Twists
Butter Squares
Peach Conserve
Coffee

MEAT & POTATOES DINNER
Stuffed Meat Rolls, page 164
Whipped Mashed Potatoes, page 99
Zucchini Casserole, page 94
Garden Salad
Peach Cobbler
Coffee or Tea

Yogo-Cheese

Double satisfaction: make homemade cheese, then enjoy the flavor.

1 quart Whole Milk Yogurt, page 14,   1/8 teaspoon salt
   or plain yogurt

Line a colander with 4 layers of white paper towels. Place yogurt in colander. Cover with more paper towels. Place colander in a pan about 2 inches deep. Refrigerate and drain 8 to 10 hours. Check occasionally to remove excess water from the pan. Carefully remove the Yogo-Cheese from the paper towels. Place in a container with a cover. Sprinkle with salt and mix well. Yogo-Cheese will keep covered in the refrigerator up to 4 weeks. Makes about 1-1/2 cups.

Variation

Sprinkle or mix in your favorite spices or herbs. Try dill weed, chives, oregano, caraway seed or mint.

Note: Yogurts which include gelatin as an ingredient cannot be used to make Yogo-Cheese.

How To Make Yogo-Cheese

1/Place yogurt in colander and cover with more paper towels. Let yogurt drain in a 2-inch-deep pan in the refrigerator 8 hours or overnight.

2/Stir in salt. Form into desired shape. Sprinkle or mix in your favorite herbs such as caraway seed, dill weed or toasted sesame seed.

Mom's Favorite Cheese Ball

No party is complete without this one!

2 cups Yogo-Cheese, page 161
1 (6-1/2-oz.) can crabmeat,
   drained and flaked
2 tablespoons lemon juice
2 tablespoons horseradish
1-1/2 tablespoons grated onion

2 teaspoons snipped chives
Dash Worcestershire sauce
1/4 teaspoon salt
1/4 cup minced black olives
Finely chopped walnuts or pecans
Assorted crackers

In a medium bowl, place Yogo-Cheese, crabmeat, lemon juice, horseradish, onion, chives, Worcestershire sauce, salt and black olives. Blend well. Refrigerate 30 minutes. Shape into a large cheese ball or individual 1-inch cheese balls. Roll in finely chopped nuts. Serve with crackers. Makes 1 large cheese ball or about 30 individual balls.

Tasty Cheese Cubes

Make these the night before the party.

1/2 cup butter or margarine
1/4 lb. sharp Cheddar cheese, grated
1/3 cup Yogo-Cheese, page 161

2 egg whites, stiffly beaten
About 1/4 loaf French bread, cut in
   1/2- to 3/4-inch cubes

Line a baking sheet with aluminum foil. Set aside. In a medium saucepan, melt butter or margarine and Cheddar cheese. Remove from heat. Stir in Yogo-Cheese. Blend well. Fold in stiffly beaten egg whites. Dip bread cubes into cheese sauce. Place on prepared baking sheet. Cover and refrigerate 8 to 10 hours. Preheat oven to 375°F (190°C). Bake 10 minutes. Serve immediately. Makes about 75 cheese cubes.

For appetizers, use Yogo-Cheese as a substitute for cream cheese.

Easy Danish Pastry

Marvelous with midmorning coffee.

2 cups all-purpose flour
3 tablespoons sugar
1/4 teaspoon salt
1/2 cup butter or margarine, softened
2 pkgs. active dry yeast

1/4 cup warm water (110°F, 45°C)
1/2 cup milk
1 egg yolk
Yogo-Cheese Filling, see below
Thin Icing, see below

Yogo-Cheese Filling:
1 cup Yogo-Cheese, page 161
3 tablespoons powdered sugar

1/2 teaspoon vanilla extract
1/8 teaspoon salt

Thin Icing:
1 cup powdered sugar
2 tablespoons plain yogurt, room temperature

In a large bowl, mix flour, sugar, salt and butter or margarine. In a small bowl, dissolve yeast in warm water. Let stand 5 minutes. Scald milk in a small saucepan. Cool to lukewarm. Beat egg yolk and blend into cooled milk. Stir dissolved yeast and milk mixture into flour mixture. Blend well. Cover and refrigerate at least 3 hours but not more than 48 hours. Dough will rise very little. Prepare Yogo-Cheese Filling; set aside. Divide dough in half. Refrigerate 1 half until ready to use. On a lightly floured surface, roll out other half of dough to an 8" x 14" rectangle. Cut into four 2-inch wide strips. Roll each strip into a rope and shape into a coil. Fill the center of each coil with 2 table-spoons Yogo-Cheese Filling. Cover and let rise in a warm place about 20 minutes until doubled in bulk. Preheat oven to 350°F (175°C). Bake 20 minutes until golden brown. Prepare Thin Icing and drizzle over warm rolls. Makes about 8 large Danish rolls.

Yogo-Cheese Filling:
Cream all ingredients in a small bowl. Blend well.

Thin Icing:
In small bowl, combine powdered sugar and yogurt. Blend well.

Nutty Cheese Log

A delightful blend of cheeses.

3/4 cup Yogo-Cheese, page 161
1 (8-oz.) carton sharp Cheddar cheese spread
1 (4-oz.) pkg. blue cheese

Few drops Tabasco® sauce
1/2 cup blanched peanuts
Assorted crackers

In a medium bowl, blend Yogo-Cheese, Cheddar cheese spread, blue cheese and Tabasco®. Refrig-erate 30 minutes. Shape into a log. Press peanuts on top of cheese log. Refrigerate 3 to 5 hours to blend flavors. Serve with crackers. Makes 1 cheese log.

Grand Marnier Soufflé

Let's celebrate!

3/4 cup sugar
2 envelopes unflavored gelatin
2 cups water
6 eggs, separated
1 cup Yogo-Cheese, page 161

1/2 cup orange juice
1/4 cup Grand Marnier liqueur
1/4 teaspoon cream of tartar
1/4 cup sugar
Shaved semisweet chocolate, for garnish

Wrap a 3-inch collar of aluminum foil around top of a 1-1/2-quart soufflé dish. Secure with tape. In a small saucepan, mix 3/4 cup sugar and gelatin. Gradually add water. Stir over low heat to dissolve gelatin. Remove from heat. Beat egg yolks in a small bowl. Blend a small amount of gelatin mixture into beaten egg yolks. Gradually add egg yolk mixture to remaining gelatin. Cook over low heat 2 to 3 minutes. In a large bowl, beat Yogo-Cheese until creamy. Gradually add gelatin and egg yolk mixture to Yogo-Cheese. Blend well. Stir in orange juice and Grand Marnier liqueur. Refrigerate until slightly thickened. In a large bowl, beat egg whites until frothy. Add cream of tartar. Gradually beat in 1/4 cup sugar 1 tablespoon at a time until stiff peaks form. Fold into chilled Yogo-Cheese mixture. Pour into prepared soufflé dish. Refrigerate 6 to 8 hours until firm. Remove foil collar before serving. Garnish with shaved chocolate. Makes 8 to 10 servings.

Stuffed Meat Rolls

Let your butcher slice the meat for these savory specialties.

1 cup Yogo-Cheese, page 161
1/2 cup breadcrumbs
2 tablespoons butter or margarine, melted
2 green onions, thinly sliced
1/2 cup chopped celery
1/4 teaspoon salt
1/8 teaspoon pepper
1/4 cup all-purpose flour
1 teaspoon salt

1/8 teaspoon pepper
2 lbs. bottom round steak,
   sliced 1/8-inch thick,
   cut into 3" x 6" pieces
2 tablespoons vegetable oil
1 (10-1/2-oz.) can beef consommé
2 teaspoons cornstarch
1 tablespoon water
1 cup plain yogurt, room temperature

Cream Yogo-Cheese in a small bowl. Add breadcrumbs, melted butter or margarine, onions, celery, 1/4 teaspoon salt and 1/8 teaspoon pepper. In a pie plate or shallow dish, combine flour, 1 teaspoon salt and 1/8 teaspoon pepper. Dredge meat slices with flour mixture. Spread evenly with Yogo-Cheese stuffing. Roll up like a jelly roll and tie with a string. Heat oil in a large skillet. Brown meat rolls evenly on all sides. Pour consommé over meat rolls. Cover and simmer 1 hour until tender, basting occasionally. Remove meat from skillet. Place on a warm platter and cut off string. Mix cornstarch with water. Stir into hot gravy. Cook and stir until thickened. Stir yogurt until creamy. Gradually blend yogurt into hot gravy. Serve immediately. Makes about 6 to 8 servings.

Yogo-Rounds

Puffy and good.

1 (4-oz.) can mushroom stems
  and pieces, drained
1 tablespoon butter or margarine
1 cup Yogo-Cheese, page 161
1 tablespoon grated onion

1/4 teaspoon Worcestershire sauce
1 egg yolk
1/4 teaspoon salt
About 36 Melba toast rounds

In a small skillet, sauté mushrooms in butter or margarine. Remove from heat. Stir in Yogo-Cheese, onion, Worcestershire sauce, egg yolk and salt. Blend well. Spread over toast rounds. Broil 2 to 3 minutes until golden. Serve hot. Makes about 36 appetizers.

Deviled Ham Appetizers

Also delicious as a sandwich spread.

1 cup Yogo-Cheese, page 161
1 (4-1/2-oz.) can deviled ham
1 teaspoon grated onion
1/2 teaspoon prepared mustard

About 36 assorted crackers
Black olive slices, for garnish
Parsley sprigs, for garnish

In a medium bowl, stir Yogo-Cheese until creamy. Blend in deviled ham, onion and mustard. Mix well. Spread on crackers. Garnish with black olive slices and parsley sprigs. Makes about 36 appetizers.

Grasshopper Torte

Be adventurous! Try this easy five-layered delight.

1 (1-lb.) pound cake
1 (7-oz.) jar marshmallow creme
1/2 cup Yogo-Cheese, page 161
2 teaspoons crème de cacao

2 tablespoons creme de menthe
1/2 cup nondairy whipped topping
1 (6-oz.) pkg. semisweet chocolate chips (1 cup)
1/4 cup plain yogurt, room temperature

Place pound cake in freezer about 1 hour for easier slicing. In a large bowl, mix marshmallow creme and Yogo-Cheese. Blend in creme de cacao and creme de menthe. Fold in whipped topping. Refrigerate 1 hour. Melt chocolate chips in top of a double boiler. Remove from heat. Stir yogurt until creamy. Blend yogurt into chocolate. Slice pound cake lengthwise into 5 horizontal layers. Spread chilled filling between each layer. Frost top and sides of cake with chocolate-yogurt mixture. Refrigerate 3 to 5 hours before serving. Makes about 8 servings.

Surprise Pork Chops

No surprise if you anticipate superb flavor!

Yogo-Cheese Stuffing, see below
6 (1- to 1-1/2-inch thick) pork chops
    with pocket slit in each
1 teaspoon salt
1/8 teaspoon pepper
1/4 cup minced onion

1 tablespoon flour
1/2 cup water
1 beef bouillon cube
Dash garlic salt
Dash pepper
1 cup plain yogurt, room temperature

Yogo-Cheese Stuffing:
1 cup Yogo-Cheese, page 161
1 tablespoon snipped chives
1/4 cup breadcrumbs

1/2 teaspoon oregano
1/8 teaspoon garlic salt
1/8 teaspoon pepper

Prepare Yogo-Cheese Stuffing. Preheat oven to 325°F (165°C). Sprinkle pork chops with salt and 1/8 teaspoon pepper. Fill each chop with about 3 tablespoons Yogo-Cheese Stuffing. Fasten with wooden picks or metal skewers. Stand chops bone-side down in a shallow baking pan. Bake 1 hour until browned and cooked. Place chops on a warm platter. Put 2 tablespoons drippings from pan into a small saucepan. Add onion and flour. Sauté until golden brown. Add water, bouillon cube, garlic salt and dash of pepper. Cook and stir until slightly thickened. Stir yogurt until creamy. Gradually blend into hot gravy. Heat to serving temperature, but do not boil. Pour gravy over chops. Makes 4 to 6 servings.

Yogo-Cheese Stuffing:
In a small bowl, stir Yogo-Cheese until creamy. Blend in chives, breadcrumbs, oregano, garlic salt and pepper. Mix well.

Artichoke Appetizers

Make the cheese mixture the night before and refrigerate it.

1 cup Yogo-Cheese, page 161
3/4 cup grated Parmesan cheese
2 tablespoons mayonnaise-style salad dressing,
    not mayonnaise

About 36 slices rye cocktail bread
1 (14-oz.) can artichoke hearts,
    drained and chopped

Preheat oven to 400°F (205°C). In a medium bowl, blend Yogo-Cheese, Parmesan cheese and salad dressing until creamy. Refrigerate until ready to serve, if desired. Spread cheese mixture on bread and top with chopped artichokes, or place chopped artichokes on bread and top with cheese mixture. Bake 5 minutes. Serve immediately. Makes about 36 appetizers.

Variation

Substitute canned chopped mushrooms or chopped black olives for the artichokes.

Creamy Yogo-Cheese Pie

A velvety texture.

Easy Graham Cracker Crust, see below
1 (8-oz.) pkg. cream cheese,
   room temperature
3 tablespoons honey

1 teaspoon vanilla extract
1 cup Yogo-Cheese, page 161
   room temperature

Easy Graham Cracker Crust:
1-1/4 cups crushed graham crackers
   (about 15 crackers)

3 tablespoons sugar
6 tablespoons butter or margarine, melted

Prepare Easy Graham Cracker Crust. In a large bowl, cream together cream cheese, honey and vanilla extract with an electric mixer on low speed. Add Yogo-Cheese a little at a time. Blend until smooth. Pour into graham cracker crust. Refrigerate 24 hours before serving. Cut into 2-inch squares. Makes about 16 pieces.

Easy Graham Cracker Crust:
In a medium bowl, mix graham cracker crumbs, sugar and butter or margarine. Press firmly into an 8-inch square pan. Refrigerate 45 minutes.

Lime Salad

Simply outstanding!

1 (8-1/2-oz.) can crushed pineapple
Water
2 (3-oz.) pkgs. lime gelatin

1 cup Yogo-Cheese, page 161
2 tablespoons powdered sugar
1/2 cup whipping cream, whipped

Generously oil a 6-cup mold. Set aside. Drain pineapple thoroughly, and reserve juice. Add enough water to pineapple juice to make 3-1/2 cups. Bring juice to a boil in a small saucepan. Dissolve gelatin in boiling liquid. Refrigerate until slightly thickened. Cream together Yogo-Cheese, powdered sugar and pineapple. Using a whisk, gradually blend Yogo-Cheese mixture into gelatin. Fold in whipped cream. Pour into prepared mold. Refrigerate until firm. Makes about 8 servings.

Swirled Strawberry Pie

Swirl Yogo-Cheese into this popular dessert.

1 quart fresh strawberries
1 cup water
1 cup granulated sugar
3 tablespoons cornstarch
Few drops red food coloring

1 cup Yogo-Cheese, page 161
1 tablespoon powdered sugar
1 (9-inch) pie shell, baked and cooled
Whipped cream, if desired

Wash and hull strawberries. In a small saucepan, crush 1 cup of the smaller berries and cook in 1 cup water about 3 minutes. Press cooked berries through a sieve. Stir together granulated sugar and cornstarch. Add to berry juice. Cook and stir until clear and thickened. Remove from heat. Stir in food coloring. Reserve 2 tablespoons Yogo-Cheese for glaze. Stir remaining Yogo-Cheese with powdered sugar until creamy. Cover bottom of pie shell with Yogo-Cheese mixture. Stand strawberries, stem-side down, over the cheese. Carefully swirl remaining 2 tablespoons Yogo-Cheese into cooled glaze giving a marbled effect. Pour glaze over berries. Refrigerate about 4 hours until firm before serving. Garnish with whipped cream, if desired. Makes about 6 servings.

How To Make Swirled Strawberry Pie

1/Cover the bottom of a baked pie shell with Yogo-Cheese and powdered sugar mixture. Stand strawberries, stem-side down, over cheese.

2/Carefully swirl 2 tablespoons Yogo-Cheese into cooled pie glaze to give a marbled effect. Pour over berries in pie shell and refrigerate until firm.

Fluffy Yogo-Cheesecake

Light as a feather and so tasty!

1 Graham Cracker Crust, page 149
2 tablespoons unflavored gelatin
1/4 cup cold water
1/2 cup milk
2 egg yolks, slightly beaten
1 cup sugar
1 teaspoon salt

Grated peel of 2 lemons
Juice of 2 lemons
2 teaspoons vanilla extract
2 cups Yogo-Cheese, page 161
2 egg whites, stiffly beaten
1 cup whipping cream, whipped

Bake Graham Cracker Crust in a spring-form pan. Set aside to cool. Soften gelatin in cold water. Mix milk, egg yolks, sugar and salt in a medium saucepan. Cook and stir until slightly thickened. Add softened gelatin and grated lemon peel. Stir to dissolve gelatin. Set aside to cool. Gradually stir lemon juice and vanilla extract into Yogo-Cheese. Gradually add gelatin mixture to Yogo-Cheese mixture, blending well. Fold in beaten egg whites and whipped cream. Pour into crust. Refrigerate 8 to 10 hours. Makes about 12 servings.

Strawberry Surprise Mold

Yogo-Cheese adds delightful flavor.

2 tablespoons unflavored gelatin
1/4 cup cold water
1 (3-oz.) pkg. strawberry-flavored gelatin
1-3/4 cups boiling water

1 tablespoon lemon juice
2 (10-oz.) pkgs. frozen sliced strawberries,
  slightly thawed
1/2 cup Yogo-Cheese, page 161

Generously oil a 5-cup ring mold. Set aside. Sprinkle unflavored gelatin over cold water in a small bowl. Let stand 5 minutes. Add strawberry gelatin and softened unflavored gelatin to boiling water. Stir to dissolve gelatins. Add lemon juice and undrained strawberries. Chill to consistency of unbeaten egg white. Pour about 1/3 of slightly thickened gelatin into prepared ring mold. Carefully spoon Yogo-Cheese around center of gelatin, keeping Yogo-Cheese away from the edges. Spoon remaining gelatin over all. Refrigerate 4 to 5 hours until set. Makes about 8 servings.

Cucumber Sandwiches

Great for the lunchbox or canapé tray.

1 large cucumber
1/2 cup Yogo-Cheese, page 161
   room temperature
2 teaspoons grated onion
1/4 teaspoon salt
Dash white pepper
Dash garlic powder

12 to 16 white, whole-wheat or
   rye bread slices
4 to 5 tablespoons butter or margarine,
   softened
Black olive slices
Parsley sprigs, for garnish

Peel cucumber. Remove seeds and grate enough cucumber to measure 1 cup. Press through a sieve and drain well. Mash Yogo-Cheese in a small bowl. Add cucumber, onion, salt, white pepper and garlic powder. Mix well. Trim crusts from bread. Spread about 1 teaspoon butter or margarine on each slice to prevent bread from becoming soggy. Spread 3 to 4 tablespoons cucumber mixture on half the bread slices. Top with black olive slices and remaining bread slices. Garnish with parsley sprigs. Refrigerate until ready to serve. Makes 6 to 8 sandwiches.

Variation

To make canapés, cut trimmed bread slices into desired shapes. Spread with butter or margarine. Top with cucumber mixture and black olive slices. Sprinkle with paprika and garnish with parsley. Makes about 50 canapés.

Mix Yogo-Cheese with a little honey and use as a spread for English muffins.

CONVERSION TO METRIC MEASURE

WHEN YOU KNOW	SYMBOL	MULTIPLY BY	TO FIND	SYMBOL
teaspoons	tsp	5	milliliters	ml
tablespoons	tbsp	15	milliliters	ml
fluid ounces	fl oz	30	milliliters	ml
cups	c	0.24	liters	l
pints	pt	0.47	liters	l
quarts	qt	0.95	liters	l
ounces	oz	28	grams	g
pounds	lb	0.45	kilograms	kg
Fahrenheit	°F	5/9 (after subtracting 32)	Celsius	C
inches	in	2.54	centimeters	cm
feet	ft	30.5	centimeters	cm

LIQUID MEASURE TO MILLILITERS

1/4 teaspoon	=	1.25 milliliters
1/2 teaspoon	=	2.5 milliliters
3/4 teaspoon	=	3.75 milliliters
1 teaspoon	=	5 milliliters
1-1/4 teaspoons	=	6.25 milliliters
1-1/2 teaspoons	=	7.5 milliliters
1-3/4 teaspoons	=	8.75 milliliters
2 teaspoons	=	10 milliliters
1 tablespoon	=	15 milliliters
2 tablespoons	=	30 milliliters

LIQUID MEASURE TO LITERS

1/4 cup	=	0.06 liters
1/2 cup	=	0.12 liters
3/4 cup	=	0.18 liters
1 cup	=	0.24 liters
1-1/4 cups	=	0.3 liters
1-1/2 cups	=	0.36 liters
2 cups	=	0.48 liters
2-1/2 cups	=	0.6 liters
3 cups	=	0.72 liters
3-1/2 cups	=	0.84 liters
4 cups	=	0.96 liters
4-1/2 cups	=	1.08 liters
5 cups	=	1.2 liters
5-1/2 cups	=	1.32 liters

FAHRENHEIT TO CELSIUS

F	C
200°	93°
225°	107°
250°	121°
275°	135°'
300°	149°
325°	163°
350°	177°
375°	191°
400°	204°
425°	218°
450°	232°
475°	246°
500°	260°

Index

Index